The Will to Punish

The Berkeley Tanner Lectures

The Tanner Lectures on Human Values were established by the American scholar, industrialist, and philanthropist Obert Clark Tanner; they are presented annually at nine universities in the United States and England. The University of California, Berkeley became a permanent host of annual Tanner Lectures in the academic year 2000–2001. This work is the eleventh in a series of books based on the Berkeley Tanner Lectures. The volume includes a revised version of the lectures that Didier Fassin presented at Berkeley in April 2016, together with the responses of the three invited commentators on that occasion—Bruce Western, Rebecca M. McLennan, David W. Garland—and a final rejoinder by Professor Fassin. The volume is edited by Christopher Kutz, who also contributes an introduction. The Berkeley Tanner Lecture Series was established in the belief that these distinguished lectures, together with the lively debates stimulated by their presentation in Berkeley, deserve to be made available to a wider audience. Additional volumes are in preparation.

Martin Jay
R. Jay Wallace
Series Editors

Volumes Published in the Series

Joseph Raz, *The Practice of Value*
Edited by R. Jay Wallace
With Christine M. Korsgaard, Robert Pippin, and Bernard Williams

Frank Kermode, *Pleasure and Change: The Aesthetics of Canon*
Edited by Robert Alter
With Geoffrey Hartman, John Guillory, and Carey Perloff

Seyla Benhabib, *Another Cosmopolitanism*
Edited by Robert Post
With Jeremy Waldron, Bonnie Honig, and Will Kymlicka

Axel Honneth, *Reification: A New Look at an Old Idea*
Edited by Martin Jay
With Judith Butler, Raymond Guess, and Jonathan Lear

Allan Gibbard, *Reconciling Our Aims: In Search of Bases for Ethics*
Edited by Barry Stroud
With Michael Bratman, John Broome, and F. M. Kamm

Derek Parfit, *On What Matters: Volumes 1 and 2*
Edited by Samuel Scheffler
With Susan Wolf, Allen Wood, Barbara Herman, and T. M. Scanlon,

Jeremy Waldron, *Dignity, Rank, and Rights*
Edited by Meir Dan-Cohen
With Wai Chee Dimock, Don Herzog, and Michael Rosen

Samuel Scheffler, *Death and the Afterlife*
Edited by Niko Kolodny
With Susan Wolf, Harry G. Frankfurt, and Seana Valentine Shiffrin

Eric L. Santner, *The Weight Of All Flesh: On the Subject-Matter of Political Economy*
Edited by Kevis Goodman
With Bonnie Honig, Peter E. Gordon, and Hent De Vries

F. M. Kamm, *The Trolley Problem Mysteries*
Edited by Eric Rakowski
With Judith Jarvis Thomson, Thomas Hurka, and Shelly Kagan

The Will to Punish

Didier Fassin

With Commentaries by
Bruce Western
Rebecca M. McLennan
David W. Garland

Edited and Introduced by
Christopher Kutz

OXFORD
UNIVERSITY PRESS

OXFORD
UNIVERSITY PRESS

Oxford University Press is a department of the University of Oxford. It furthers the University's objective of excellence in research, scholarship, and education by publishing worldwide. Oxford is a registered trade mark of Oxford University Press in the UK and certain other countries.

Published in the United States of America by Oxford University Press
198 Madison Avenue, New York, NY 10016, United States of America.

CIP data is on file at the Library of Congress
ISBN 978–0–19–088858–9

A French version of Didier Fassin's text has been published under the title *Punir: Une passion contemporaine* (Le Seuil, 2017).

Contents

# *Acknowledgments*

Delivering the Tanner Lectures on Human Values is an immense honor, and succeeding the distinguished scholars and intellectuals who have previously given them is a great privilege. Anthropologists and sociologists are certainly not the most numerous in this prestigious list, and as it is the first time that someone from these disciplines has this honor at the University of California, Berkeley, the challenge is even greater.

I am therefore especially grateful to Chancellor Nicholas Dirks and Professor Martin Jay as well as the chair and vice chair, respectively, of the Tanner Committee for their invitation to develop these untimely meditations on punishment, if I may dare such reference to the author who has accompanied my reflection as I was preparing them. I also want to express my gratitude to Professors David Garland, Rebecca McLennan, and Bruce Western for having agreed to provide comments on my lectures; I could not have imagined a better set of discussants. Several colleagues and friends have made various contributions at different stages of the elaboration of this book, in particular Linda Bosniak, José Brunner, Bernard Harcourt, Axel Honneth, Jaeeun Kim, Christopher Kutz, Thomas Lemke, Allegra McLeod, Ayşe Parla, Yves Sintomer, Felix Trautmann, Peter Wagner, and Linda Zerilli, for which I am appreciative. In the preparation of the manuscript, I have also benefited from Laura McCune's copyediting and Anne-Claire Defossez's remarks.

But since this theoretical reflection is based on ten years of empirical research on police, justice, and prisons in France, as part of an Advanced Grant from the European Research Council, I must finally acknowledge my debt toward all those who have rendered my work possible and have nourished it with their knowledge and experience: officers, commissioners, judges, lawyers, guards, wardens, parole counselors, social workers, health professionals, public officials, politicians, activists, prisoners, citizens.

I dedicate this essay to my father who passed away as I was preparing my lectures and whose inspiration is probably more profound than I even realize.

Didier Fassin
January 2017

Contributors

DIDIER FASSIN is the James D. Wolfensohn Professor of Social Science at the Institute for Advanced Study in Princeton and a director of studies at the École des Hautes Études en Sciences Sociales in Paris. Anthropologist, sociologist, and physician, he has worked in Senegal, South Africa, Ecuador, and France in the domain of political and moral anthropology. His recent work includes an ethnography of the French state based on fieldwork with the police, justice, and prison systems, which he conducted as part of his Advanced Grant of the European Research Council, and a theoretical reflection on the public presence of the social science, which he presented in his recipient lecture for the Gold Medal in Anthropology at the Swedish Royal Academy of Arts and Sciences. He recently authored *Humanitarian Reason: A Moral History of the Present* (2011), *Enforcing Order: An Ethnography of Urban Policing* (2013), *Prison Worlds: An Ethnography of the Carceral Condition* (2016), and the forthcoming *Life: A Critical User's Manual.*

DAVID GARLAND is Arthur T. Vanderbilt Professor of Law and a professor of sociology at New York University. His books include *The Welfare State: A Very Short Introduction* (2016), *Peculiar Institution: America's Death Penalty in an Age of Abolition* (2010), *The Culture of Control: Crime and Social Order in Contemporary Society* (2001), *Punishment and Modern Society: A Study in Social Theory* (1990), and *Punishment and Welfare: A History of Penal Strategies* (1985; new ed. 2017).

CHRISTOPHER KUTZ is C. William Maxeiner Distinguished Professor of Law in the Jurisprudence and Social Policy Program (Berkeley

Law School), at U.C. Berkeley. He works in the areas of the philosophy of criminal law and international law, as well as moral and political philosophy. His books include *On War and Democracy* (2016) and *Complicity: Ethics and Law for a Collective Age* (2000).

Rebecca McLennan is an associate professor of history at U.C. Berkeley, where she specializes in nineteenth- and twentieth-century American history. Her books include *Becoming America* (with David Henkin, 2014) and *The Crisis of Imprisonment: Protest, Politics, and the Making of the American Penal State, 1776–1941* (2008).

Bruce Western is the Daniel and Florence Guggenheim Professor of Criminal Justice Policy at the John F. Kennedy School of Government and a professor of sociology at Harvard University. He is a specialist both in sociological methods and in the sociology of the American punishment system. His books include *Punishment and Inequality in America* (2006) and *Between Class and Market: Postwar Unionization in the Capitalist Democracies* (1997).

The Will to Punish

Introduction

CHRISTOPHER KUTZ

In 1887 Friedrich Nietzsche famously offered a catalog of the multifarious uses of punishment:

> Punishment as a means of rendering harmless, of preventing further harm. Punishment as recompense to the injured party for the harm done. . . . Punishment as the isolation of a disturbance of equilibrium, so as to guard against any further spread of the disturbance. Punishment as a means of inspiring fear of those who determine and execute the punishment. Punishment as a kind of repayment for the advantages the criminal has enjoyed hitherto. . . . Punishment as the expulsion of a degenerate element. . . . Punishment as a festival, namely as the rape and mockery of a finally defeated enemy. . . . Punishment as payment of a fee, stipulated by the power that protects the wrongdoer from the excesses of revenge. . . . Punishment as a declaration of war and a war measure against an enemy of the peace, of the law, of order, of the authorities.[1]

Nietzsche's aim was to disrupt what he regarded as an unreflective Judeo-Christian moralization of punishment, a process then rationalized by Immanuel Kant in the Enlightenment as the expression of a kind of respect owed to the wrongdoer. Punishment, Nietzsche insisted, is not the product of a metaphysics of right meeting wrong, nor of the operation of the categorical imperative. Rather the practices of punishment represent impulses and drives that outrun their ethical rationalization. Any philosophical justification of punishment is a matter of the tail wagging the dog.

In this volume, revising Tanner Foundation lectures given at Berkeley in April 2016, Didier Fassin embeds Nietzsche's aperçu in a rich anthropological and sociological context, extending Nietzsche's genealogy into a critical examination of modern penality in the United States and France. Fassin's aim is to illuminate the gap between what we believe we are doing when we punish and what in fact we do. He begins, like Nietzsche, with a philosophical target: the influential account of punishment provided by the eminent English legal philosopher H. L. A. Hart in his "Prolegomenon to the Principles of Punishment." Hart defined legal punishment as involving (a) the infliction of unpleasant consequences (b) for a violation of legal rules (c) on an actual or suspected offender, (d) intentionally administered by (e) an authority of the legal system so empowered to act.[2] Hart's aim was principally to set in place a definition of punishment that would not beg any questions with respect to the long-running debate between retributivists and utilitarians, and secondarily to make use of a distinction between those principles that justify punishment of offenders (as opposed to some other treatment) and principles restricting punishment only to those who have committed an offense.[3] But, as Fassin remarks, Hart's definition is hardly philosophically innocent; it seems to presuppose the legitimacy of the practice it defines, in terms of justified suffering for a legal violation. And indeed Hart's principal foil in his prolegomenon is neither the retributivist nor the utilitarian seeking to score easy points with a definition, but the reformer, seeking to replace a system of punishment altogether with a model of therapeutic treatment. His goal, in other words, is to recenter debate around the core example of state punishment, thereby to offer the best account of its structure and justification.[4]

What Fassin shows us in these lectures is how a focus on what Hart claims as the core instance of punishment obscures the vast web of our penal practices, which lie far in excess of suffering inflicted only on offenders; and how that definitional focus makes too easy the justification of social violence that is meted out more by reference to economic and ethnoracial status than to moralized considerations of harm. For if we accept Hart's invitation and focus only on the core instance of punishment allocated after arrest and a duly procedural trial, limited to the terms of the judge's sentence, we will be blind to the way penality operates throughout our social world, in both its extent and its aims. We need, instead, to follow Fassin for a look across the borders of time, space, and—especially—class and race to answer the central questions he poses: What, why, and whom do we punish? Notably the answers Fassin offers are those of an anthropologist, not a philosopher: we (in power) define crimes in order to punish; we punish in order to maintain status hierarchies; and we punish those whose existence or behavior threatens status hierarchies. But even this description is too calculating, too rational. Hence Fassin's titular paraphrase of Nietzsche: we punish out of will, not intention, a will to render suffering.

Many readers of these lectures will be familiar with Michel Foucault's *Discipline and Punish* and Michelle Alexander's *The New Jim Crow*, and hence also with the argument that penal policy often does much more than it claims, in securing lines of power and privilege and, in the case of Alexander's book, in maintaining white supremacy.[5] Fassin amplifies their accounts by leading us on an anthropologist's global tour of the carceral economy. We find our baseline with a stop guided by Malinowski in the Trobriand Islands of the Pacific, where wrongs among the Kima'i were met with rituals and gossip; punishment, such as it was, was self-administered, even for serious violations of local norms. We then move to a very different island, Rikers, where New York City's jailed population are kept, including a boy arrested for a crime he almost certainly did not commit and held three years without trial, during which he suffered great abuse, leading to a catastrophic breakdown and suicide. We thus have two poles: wrongs without punishment and punishment without wrongs. Between these two lies an especially interesting landscape of penal practice, with many examples drawn from etymology and ancient and medieval historiography. But

Fassin's own anthropological work in French banlieues, trial courts, prisons, and jails is the core of his case. Take the example of a Roma man whom Fassin discusses in Lecture Two, arrested for driving without a license. Fassin shows that his is a case of someone already economically marginalized, who takes the only work he can find, as a delivery driver. As someone frequently on the roads, he is statistically subject to extra police scrutiny and automatic speed enforcement; inevitably the driving violations pile up, and with them the fines that greatly exceed his ability to pay them. The result is a cycle of incarceration, domestic stress, and temptations of further crime offered while in prison. Here is a case where crime seems to be the product of punishment, of a system that begins with an assertion of guilt and then finding crimes to fit.[6] Though Fassin's observation arises in France, it mirrors, as he says, a very typical American practice, including the dimension of ethnic stratification, poignantly documented in the U.S. Justice Department's investigation of policing for profit among the poor in Ferguson, Missouri.[7]

Indeed although Americans have come to see our justice system as exceptional in its violence and racial skew, one lesson of Fassin's lectures is that the flaws of the American system are widely shared. Fassin mounts the case in Lecture Three of a young French man with Senegalese parents, whose record of petty theft and life in the housing projects makes him a frequent target of police stop-and-frisks and who comes into court accused of resisting arrest and "insulting" the police during custody. (Fassin has observed how such charges can be manufactured by police when raiding a project.) The young man is taciturn in court and his lawyer uninspired. But because the police witness does not appear, there is no trial or sentencing, only a nominally exceptional decision to hold the young man in jail until a trial can be held, to retroactively affirm the punishment already meted out. Fassin contrasts this with the case of another young man, white and middle class, accused of violently sexually assaulting his partner. There is no dispute about the facts, but the defendant is humble and presents himself well, announcing his remorse. He receives a suspended six-month sentence.[8] Again, what might seem a philosophical unity, crime/punishment, is revealed to be a tangled network indirectly linking sanctions with class stratification. Moreover, as Fassin argues, the penality network dynamically strengthens itself: modern states are becoming more punitive in lockstep with their tendency toward increasing social inequality.[9] What has dropped out is the individual idealized in criminal justice—the agent who responsibly chooses to violate a legal norm and then is punished on its basis. Or rather, as Fassin suggests, the individual remains, but as the protagonist of an illusion whose deeds and deserts convey legitimacy on a system that seeks to obscure the structural violence it wreaks.

When Fassin presented his lectures, he was joined by an exceptionally distinguished panel of commentators. David Garland, a professor of sociology and law at NYU, is widely known as one of the leading theoretical criminologists of the Anglophone world. Rebecca McLennan, a professor of history at Berkeley, is the author of a groundbreaking examination of the centrality of prison labor to the American penal system. And Bruce Western, a professor of sociology at Harvard, is one of the nation's leading sociologists focusing on the intersection of criminal justice and racial and economic inequality. The result was one of the most successful Tanner Lectures in my experience; whereas lecturers and commentators can sometimes find themselves locking horns from the start, Fassin himself incorporated his commentators' work into his own argument, so that the discussion among the four was an unusually constructive adumbration of shared themes and observations. These conversations took place in the usual Tanner format, with one commentator (Western) addressing Fassin's first lecture, then Garland and McLennan addressing the second lecture together. The third day involved a collective discussion as well as more comments by all three. The comments published here reflect the prepared remarks given on all three days and are largely published as delivered.

Western's comments reflect the breadth of his pioneering research on the way the American penal system has affected the "life course" of African American men. He focuses on the twin facts that structure a distressing portion of African American men, particularly those without a high school degree: they are both the object of the criminal justice system (with as high as a 70 percent lifetime chance of imprisonment) and its basis, as vastly disproportionate victims of violent crime, especially homicide. Western details his own research exposing the violent medium in which those subject to imprisonment are raised from early childhood. The ubiquity of nonstate violence also destabilizes the philosopher's picture of an individual choosing to act criminally, for that picture presupposes a background of social order; put another way, we cannot understand state violence without seeing its entanglement in nonstate violence. Western also calls for more attention to the nature of poverty, which is deeply associated with conditions of extensive nonstate violence. While reformers have long raised the question whether policies aimed at alleviating poverty would be a better way to avoid crime, Western goes further, to note that the dehumanizing processes that allow a rich society to tolerate and perpetuate poverty are the same processes that allow it to ignore or underplay the effects of its penal system on that same population. Western offers a proposal for a positive vision that can shape reform of the system that Fassin so well critiques: a commitment to social justice (alleviating inequality), the dignity of all those within the justice system, and the Benthamite ideal of parsimony in punishment, doling out suffering when and only insofar as it will accomplish social goals.

McLennan urges Fassin to pay more attention to the details of American penal history. She notes that his account of the American system essentially jumps from the beginning of the nineteenth century and the invention of the modern penitentiary in Philadelphia and Auburn, Alabama, to the chaos of Rikers Island. What is missing, according to McLennan, is an account of how the "political and moral economies of punishment change over time."

In particular she urges an examination of how, concurrent with the penitentiary, penal justice was still exercised in the town square and the roads of America by lynch mobs and slave patrols and how the economic model of the slave plantation was extended throughout the American penal system. McLennan also notes that a problem with a Nietzsche-influenced "theology" of the punishment system might be vulnerable, when applied to America, because of the difficulty in representing the Judeo-Christian tradition as a coherent unity rather than an intensely contentious body of arguments, especially within Protestantism. Some Protestants, she observes, were critical of the social isolation of prisoners within the penitentiary system because they regarded punishment as a communal affair; others, part of the Christian progressivism at the end of the nineteenth century, rejected both pain and servitude as suitable punishments. McLennan also notes that an account of gender disparities in punishment would be helpful—both between men and women and between France and the United States, which punishes a much greater proportion of its female population than France, or indeed than anywhere else in the world.

Garland shares Fassin's normative concerns with the extent, unruliness, and sheer irrationality of the penal state. But he raises an important concern, which echoes Western's discussion of criminal violence. In Fassin's telling, there seems to be only one real agent in the story, namely the state (or the power system), while criminals are rendered as objects made and tossed about by the system. In part this is a product of Fassin's interest in structure rather than the individual, and in part it is a product of the special role drug cases play in his case studies—drug cases, after all, feature conduct that is socially approved for some substances (notably alcohol) and disapproved for others (marijuana, disappearingly; cocaine), and so they are prime material for an argument that penality is a state practice of labeling some acts as criminal and then unleashing violent and arbitrary processes in relation to those acts. But, says Garland, this is to lose sight of the role that actual violent crime plays in the penal system; one cannot adequately critique the processes of criminal justice if one pretends or ignores the acts of violence by individuals that set it in motion.[10] Of course, as Western too argues, understanding violent crime through the anthropologist's and sociologist's lenses will also tend to correct the philosophical view Fassin targets.

Garland offers optimism in his final remarks. Fassin's argument against Hart's definition, and the general philosophical project of rationalizing punishment, is highly persuasive in showing that the philosophical project largely fails to make contact with social reality. But, says Garland, the point of Hart's definition was to help stabilize a discussion meant to be critical of existing practice, even if it necessarily supposes the legitimacy of some ideal penal system. Should we, he asks, discard the ideal of a legally regulated system of punishment? We can condemn in direct moral terms the abuses of Rikers Island, the targeting and harassment of minority members of the community, lynch mobs. But our critique is all the more powerful when we can show that such acts and processes are also illegal. Law's demand that punishment be meted out only on clear evidence of wrongdoing, and only within proper channels, might strike us today as less than inspiring. Garland suggests we would be unwise to dispense with it, even in our role as critics.

Fassin contributes a response to his commentators in this volume. While his response speaks for itself, I would note only the important normative and methodological difference he insists upon. Although all four discussants agree about the excessive and unchecked violence and discrimination present in the penal systems Fassin discusses, he insists, beyond the others, on recovering an understanding of punishment not from the formal structures that claim to channel and so legitimate it but from ethnography and genealogy. Western and Garland in particular are inclined to accept a Hartian definition of punishment, and then decry excesses in relation to that definition. But Fassin's point is that we perpetuate a dangerous illusion if we do not see that penality, in its very nature, is unconfined by principle and limits.

Fassin's Tanner Lectures were delivered at a moment of relative optimism in criminal justice policy. Because of the growing and broadening recognition of the damage done by mass incarceration and the increasing visibility among white elites of police violence against African American men, criminal justice policies had begun to shift at both state and federal levels. The incarcerated population of the U.S. had begun to decline from its historic high (even as it remained a global outlier), federal orders were issued to avoid the use of for-profit private prisons, court decisions had caused reductions in state prison overcrowding, and disparities in crack versus powdered cocaine sentencing were eliminated.[11] As Fassin writes, Barack Obama became the first sitting president to visit a maximum-security prison, not to gloat but to express his support for ameliorative criminal justice policies; among Obama's final acts in office were the commutations of more than 1,700 nonviolent drug offenders in federal prison. More generally, increased recognition of the deep flaws of the system was beginning to inspire and support effective movements for social justice.

By the time of this publication, the national landscape has changed dramatically. We now have an Attorney General apparently intent on resurrecting all parts of the War on Crime and the War on Drugs to their full ferocity and irrationality. Private prison stocks soared with the election results, and their use has been restored. Prosecutors have been instructed to seek maximum sentences in drug cases. Federal review of police departments for civil rights violations has been rescinded. And the U.S. presidency itself is now inhabited by a man who urges police officers to commit more violence during arrest, not less.[12] A Congress that seemed momentarily awake, across party lines, to the problem of mass incarceration has returned to deliberate avoidance of the issue. History, it seems, is making the insights and truths of these lectures all the more important, even as it makes them crueler to bear.

Notes

1. Friedrich Nietzsche, *On the Genealogy of Morals* (1886), trans. Walter Kaufmann (New York: Vintage Press, reissue 1989), second essay, sec. 13.

2. H. L. A. Hart, "Prolegomenon to the Principles of Punishment," in *Punishment and Responsibility*, 2nd ed. (Oxford: Oxford University Press, 2008), 7.

3. Hart himself aimed to join what he saw as valuable in retributive theories, namely their categorical exclusion of punishing the innocent, with the instrumental rationality of utilitarian accounts of the justifying aim of punishment, namely deterrence and incapacitation. His complete theory of punishment treats a limited model of penal deterrence, constrained by innocence and excuse, as a fair and liberty-protecting system of social order, consistent with respect for autonomous political actors.

4. Whatever one thinks of the merits of Hart's (and many midcentury liberals') concern with the totalitarian possibilities of psychiatry's expanding empire, it is noteworthy that he seems more concerned with preserving a philosophical case for punishment than holding the whole practice open to philosophical skepticism.

5. Michel Foucault, *Discipline and Punish* (1975; New York: Vintage Press, 1995), original title *Surveiller et punir*; Michelle Alexander, *The New Jim Crow* (New York: New Press, 2010).

6. There is a strong echo here of Nietzsche's "Pale Criminal" in *Also Sprach Zarathustra*, who commits crimes in order to assuage a preexisting guilt: the police state begins with a quantum of guilt, which it then distributes by discovering "crimes."

7. U.S. Department of Justice, Civil Rights Division, "Investigation of the Ferguson Police Department," March 4, 2015, https://www.justice.gov/sites/default/files/opa/press-releases/attachments/2015/03/04/ferguson_police_department_report.pdf.

8. As Fassin notes, this is odd, since the statutory sentence for sexual assault in France is five years, extended to fifteen if the assault involves penetration and wounds, as in the present case. It seems apparent that social privilege plays more of a role in sentencing than formal legal requirements. This, again, mirrors substantial and notorious racial disparities in American law. The comparison with

France is difficult because French law (grounded in republican values) prohibits the collection of racial data, but Fassin estimates that nearly 80 percent of those in the French penal system are ethnoracial minorities.

9. The juxtaposition in contemporary America, as Fassin states, is especially striking: the federal government has essentially ended the individual prosecution of high-level financial fraud even as it continues to prosecute the War on Drugs against low-level individuals.

10. John Pfaff's *Locked In* (New York: Basic Books, 2017) provides a data-rich argument that increased charging and sentencing of violent crime, not drugs, is the prime driver of mass incarceration at the state level, where most prisoners are found.

11. For a cautious celebration of the changing legal landscape, see Jonathan Simon, *Mass Incarceration on Trial* (New York: New Press, 2014).

12. Cleve R. Wootson Jr. and Mark Berman, "U.S. Police Chiefs Blast Trump for Endorsing 'Police Brutality,'" *Washington Post*, July 30, 2017.

The Will to Punish

Prologue: A Tale of Two Societies

In his 1926 essay, "Primitive Crime and Its Punishment," often considered the foundational text of legal anthropology, Bronislaw Malinowski recounts an episode that occurred during his fieldwork in the Trobriand Islands and profoundly influenced his views on law and order in "savage society," as he calls it.[1] "One day an outbreak of wailing and a great commotion told me that a death had occurred somewhere in the neighborhood. I was informed that Kima'i, a young lad of my acquaintance, of sixteen or so, had fallen from a coco-nut palm and killed himself." Upon his arrival at the village where the mourning and burial took place, the anthropologist noted several peculiar facts, such as an unusual hostility among the participants, but he did not pay attention to them, as he was more interested in the unfolding of the ceremony. Only later was he able to comprehend the meaning of these tensions: the youth had actually committed suicide after his incestuous liaison with the daughter of his mother's sister had been discovered. Indeed, as is the case in totemic societies, having a sexual relationship with and, even worse, getting married to someone of one's own clan was deemed by Trobrianders the most serious infringement of their moral system. "Nothing arouses a greater horror than the breach of this prohibition," writes Malinowski, who adds, however, that it is at least "the ideal of native law" because "when it comes to the application to real life, things take a different complexion." As his long-term presence in the field allowed him to observe, in practice, although the breach of the "rules of exogamy" was not uncommon, it was reproved but tolerated. "Public opinion is lenient, though decidedly hypocritical," comments the anthropologist.

So what did happen that could account for the boy's tragic gesture? In fact the discovery of the incestuous liaison had initially given rise to the usual silent disapproval by the members of the community, until the day when another young man who wanted to marry the girl came forward publicly. After having ineffectively threatened his rival with sorcery, he went out to the rival's village and hurled abuse at him, accusing him of incest. For the unfortunate Kima'i, the only possible remedy for such a public shaming was to take his own life. "The next morning, he put on his festive attire and ornamentation, climbed a coco-nut palm and addressed the community." After having bid farewell to the members of his clan and moaned aloud in a customary manner, he jumped from the tree and killed himself. A moment later a fight broke out and the discarded lover was wounded. The resulting tensions between the two clans explained the palpable animosity during the funeral.

However, for the anthropologist, the most significant element of the incident was not the suicide as such but rather the rarity of such acts compared with the banality of endogamic love affairs among Trobrianders. Most of the time what his informants described as the most horrific deed they could imagine did not receive any particular retribution when it actually occurred, as long as a certain discretion was maintained. Gossip was the rule, condemnation the exception. For those who felt personally injured, rituals invoking supernatural forces sufficed to undo the evil of the incest. According to Malinowski, this treatment contradicted the common belief shared by many among his colleagues that traditional societies were governed by strict norms, which their members slavishly obeyed for fear of grave sanctions. Conversely people invented and transmitted ways to circumvent the apparently rigid law, seeming content with a vague reprobation and convenient magic, which, by avoiding conflicts, served to preserve its social order while reminding of its moral code—an analysis in accordance with the anthropologist's functionalist inclination. Only when such situations turned into public scandals, thus revealing the failure of conservation strategies, did they generate a more radical reaction: suicide. However, even in this uncommon event the sanction belonged to a moral scenography quite remote from the usual images of repressive norms and barbarous chastisements: it was a self-inflicted sentence viewed as expiation or protest rather than retribution.

Almost a hundred years later, on the other side of the world, Jennifer Gonnerman, a writer and journalist, published an article titled "Before the Law," which revealed to a broad audience the harsh reality of the penal system in the United States. In it she recounts the biography of a young man from the Bronx named Kalief Browder who spent more than a thousand days in the dreaded jail of Rikers Island for a crime he denied having committed and for which he was never taken to court.[2] Four years earlier, at the age of sixteen, as he was walking home with a friend one evening, the two adolescents were suddenly surrounded by several police cars. "An officer said that a man had just reported that they had robbed him. 'I didn't rob anybody,' Browder replied. 'You can check my pockets.'" He was searched, as was his friend. The police did not find anything. After the police returned to their car, where the plaintiff was waiting, they came back with a new version, according to which the offense had actually happened two weeks before. The two boys were handcuffed and taken in for questioning at the precinct, where they were locked in a holding cell. The next day they were brought to a courtroom, where they learned that they were charged with robbery, grand larceny, and assault for having stolen a Mexican immigrant's backpack. They both maintained their innocence, but while his friend was released awaiting trial, Browder was detained because at the time he was on probation for pleading guilty to being an accomplice in a misdemeanor. The bail was set at three thousand dollars, a sum out of reach for his mother, who was raising seven children alone, five of whom had been, like himself, adopted. He was therefore transferred to the infamous and overcrowded jail on Rikers Island, where some six hundred male adolescents were confined in the "notoriously grim" center for minors controlled by gangs and deemed to be a "place with a deep-seated culture of violence" among both officers and inmates.

Two months later Browder was indicted by a grand jury. As he refused to plead guilty, he was taken back to prison. During the following three years he was brought to the courtroom dozens of times, but his case could never be heard because of technical problems, the unpreparedness of the file, or the unavailability of one of the protagonists of the justice system. "These guys were just playing with my case," he later commented. Although the so-called ready rule of the state of New York stipulates that, if a felony case is not brought to trial within six months after arraignment, charges should be dismissed, the repeated adjournments rendered this rule inapplicable. On several occasions the prosecutor offered Browder a guilty plea in exchange for a minor charge, and the court-appointed lawyer encouraged him to accept it, but he never did. Toward the end of his stay in jail, the judge even told him she would immediately release him if he pleaded guilty. Were he to refuse he would instead remain incarcerated until his trial. As had been the case each time he was proposed such a deal, he maintained his innocence. This attitude was rather exceptional. The previous year only 165 felony cases went to trial in the Bronx, whereas almost four thousand ended up as guilty pleas.

Meanwhile the conditions of life in prison were becoming harsher, between harassment by guards and attacks by prisoners. One night the correctional officers lined up a group of inmates to find out who had been involved in a fight and beat them up one after the other. Then, as several youths were badly hurt, they told them that if they went to the clinic and revealed what had happened to them, they would be sent to solitary confinement in retaliation.

Injured and bloodied, they all returned in silence to their cells. Solitary confinement was a common penalty there: more than one-fourth of the minors were restricted to such punitive cells on any given day. On several occasions Browder experienced it, the first time after a scuffle with a prisoner. In total he served two-thirds of his time in solitary confinement. His brother had told him that it could be a way to escape the pressure of other prisoners in the crammed fifty-bed dormitories. But he changed his mind when, during a visit, he noticed on his younger sibling's body traces of the brutality endured and food deprivation. Once, Browder had words with an officer, who, the next morning, as he was taking the young man handcuffed to the shower, knocked him down, smashed his face on the floor, and punched him viciously. Another time he was assaulted, pummeled, and kicked by a group of inmates in the presence of guards, who intervened half-heartedly. The video footages of the two incidents were later released, revealing the violence of the beatings. Not surprisingly, submitted to this arbitrary violent regime and having lost hope in a solution to his legal case, Browder became more withdrawn and depressed. He tried various times to commit suicide, especially after being told about new adjournments of his case.

Finally, a few days after he turned twenty, on his thirty-first hearing, the judge told him that the charges were dismissed as his accuser had returned to his country and could no longer be found. The young man was freed, went back home, resumed his studies, took a computer course, and vainly looked for a job. After the publication of Gonnerman's article, his case became famous. Prominent politicians used it to promote reforms of the judiciary system. Celebrities visited him and tried to help him. An anonymous donor paid his tuition for the local community college. Yet the young man was unable to get used to his new existence. He kept telling his relatives and friends about the abuses during his incarceration. "I'm mentally scarred right now. Because there are certain things that changed about me and they might not go back." His psychic health progressively deteriorated. He isolated himself in his bedroom, felt increasingly uncomfortable in the presence of people, and began to think that he was under surveillance. He was hospitalized twice in psychiatric wards. "I feel like I was robbed of my happiness," he once commented to Gonnerman. On June 6, 2015, two years after his release from prison, he hanged himself.

Why juxtapose these two cases, apparently so dissimilar, except for the fact that they both concern sixteen-year-old youths whose lives tragically end in suicide? Beyond their obvious distance in time and space—there is a priori little in common between the inhabitants of a Pacific island in the early twentieth century and the residents of a New York City borough at the beginning of the twenty-first—they are stories of crime and punishment that profoundly challenge our common understanding of what punishing means in its relation to crime. Habitual assumptions about punishment are that it is a retribution, or the infliction of a pain, on an offender, or someone supposed to have committed a wrongdoing, for a legal or moral offense, and that for the punishment to be legitimate it has to be both grounded on a legal or moral basis and appropriate in relation and proportion to the crime. This apparent self-evidence, which connects the crime and its punishment, is also widely accepted by moral philosophers and legal scholars, even if they refine its terms, complicate its qualification, and dispute its implications. Yet neither Malinowski's nor Gonnerman's account really matches this characterization. Instead they broaden and shift it. They are partially in excess of and partially outside the framework provided by commonsense assumptions and theoretical discussions.

In the case of Kima'i, there is a crime but no punishment. The violation of the exogamic law is acknowledged; it is even the transgression that, in principle, inspires the highest degree of aversion. According to the anthropologist's experience, however, it does not lead to any form of retribution. The initial and most common reaction of the group is quasi-indifference: merely gossip expressing reprobation. Then, if someone—the suitor in particular—feels personally injured, supernatural powers may be mobilized: spells, rituals, and black magic mostly destined to remedy the wrong done. But there is no punishment as such. Similar observations have been reported in other traditional societies. For instance, if incest occurs among the Yap of Micronesia, David Schneider explains, "diffuse sanctions in the form of disapproval and shunning are applied" and "the guilty pair are not ostracized, but only whispered about"; not only is there "no formal action against the transgressors," but the group even reacts "to prevent the punishment from occurring."[3] According to Malinowski, these practices constitute "a well-established system of evasion" that allows the group to reconcile the articulation of a formal rule and the banality of its actual violation. They are "completely efficient in undoing the bad results of clan incest," thus preserving the social order without questioning the moral order. Only in the rare event of a failure of these procedures, especially when a scandal leads to a situation that becomes unbearable for the group, does the resolution of the crisis call for a more radical response, namely the suicide of the transgressor.

Still, such a gesture must not be interpreted as a punishment: it is not imposed but chosen; it is conceived not as a sanction but as an expiation to repair the disorder elicited and a protest against the insult suffered. It is a question of honor, not guilt. One should therefore avoid the error committed by Keith Otterbein, who, in his "cross-cultural study of capital punishment," quotes at length the case of the unfortunate Kima'i as an illustration of his controversial thesis according to which this extreme retribution exists in all societies.[4] Beyond its ideological presuppositions and political implications, this assumption, which some have interpreted as an attempt to justify ethnologically the practice of the death penalty in the United States, proceeds from a scientific misunderstanding since Malinowski himself insists on several occasions that "the immediate and real cause of the suicide was the moment of insult" and that "suicide is certainly not a means of administering justice."

In other words, the youth's death is not a self-inflicted punishment for an admitted fault but an act of atonement and revolt, the former being intended for his clan whose peace he has threatened, and the latter being directed against his accuser for having led him to this tragic end.

In sum, the idea that a crime, and perhaps even the worst one, calls for a punishment cannot be regarded as a general and universal truth. This assertion signifies more than the banal relativist affirmation that punishment takes distinct forms in different societies. It is a statement on what we consider to be self-evident about the necessary moral and legal link between crime and punishment, namely the principle that any violation of the rule should be punished.

In the case of Browder, conversely, there is a punishment but no crime. One can certainly argue that there was a reasonable suspicion based on the allegations of the accuser, who affirmed that he had recognized his aggressors, and on the existence of antecedents, which suggested a possible profile of delinquent youth. However, this suspicion was the justification to move the case to the courts but not to decide to send the young defendant to jail. His imprisonment was not the direct consequence of the alleged crime, since his friend was left free. The remand had two justifications. First, the boy was on probation, for which the suspected offense meant a violation. Second, the judge set a bail, the amount of which substantially exceeded the financial capacity of a poor household. Thus incarceration did not result from the commission of the crime or the suspicion of it, but from the conjunction of legal mechanisms and economic constraints, the latter being the determining factor: had the sum requested been lower or the family's economic situation been better, the boy could have awaited the trial at home. This reflects a major trend in judiciary practices in the United States. In twenty years the proportion of pretrial releases including financial conditions has increased by 50 percent and the bail amount has more than doubled.[5] The suspects' resources have thus become, independently of the seriousness of the alleged offenses, a crucial factor of discrimination in the decisions to send them to jail awaiting their trial.

But one can also question the reality of the suspicion itself. In view of the imprecisions and variations in the accuser's versions, it is probably less the elements available regarding the offense than Browder's socioracial characteristics and criminal record that weighed upon the decisions of the officers, the judge, and the jury. Moreover, in such cases the doubt that should prevail at the beginning of the procedure and benefit the suspect during the trial increasingly fades away due to the massive resort to plea bargains, whereby prosecutors negotiate with the defendant an agreement to plead guilty to lesser charges. The admission thus obtained replaces the missing evidence. Within three decades the proportion of all federal criminal charges leading to trial has decreased from one out of five to one out of thirty: 97 percent of cases are currently settled in a discretionary manner by prosecutors who coerce plea bargains by threatening to charge the defendants with the most serious offenses if they do not accept a guilty plea. Of the 2.2 million convicted inmates, it is estimated that more than 2 million have been sentenced without trial as a result of a plea bargain; although it is impossible to know the proportion of innocent persons among those who have pled guilty, studies of people who have later been exonerated show that one out of ten had made such a deal.[6] This is precisely what Browder insisted on refusing, even when he was offered an immediate release if he confessed his crime; desperate but unwavering, he continued to claim his innocence and returned to his horrific carceral world. In fact, by that time the prosecutor and the judge had probably begun to have doubts, if not about his guilt, at least about the possibility of establishing it, as the plaintiff had disappeared. For them, the admission of the offense, even coerced, would have provided an honorable ending to the case. But the young man did not give them this satisfaction. They consequently had to free him after one thousand days spent in jail without having been tried, sentenced, or even convicted.

Yet that this long imprisonment should be interpreted as a punishment certainly needs to be argued. Indeed one can consider that by sending the young man to jail the judge simply wanted to make sure that he would not endanger others and would appear at the various stages of the legal procedure, although there was little evidence that these were potential risks. Technically the remand is in effect a preventive measure. But it is difficult to imagine that the judge could ignore the harsh conditions on Rikers Island, which have been documented by various official reports and journalistic accounts, especially regarding the adolescents' ward. From her perspective, the decision to confine the boy there supposed a conscious infliction of pain and therefore a belief that, being guilty, he deserved such retribution. Besides, in her view the incarceration might even have led him to admit his crime so as to shorten his suffering, which amounts to considering this ordeal a form of torture to obtain a confession. However, even under the hypothesis that the incarceration is an anticipated punishment—and it is well known that in such uncertain cases the sentence often corresponds to the exact time spent in remand, thus confirming its punitive character—one can still question the relation of proportionality between the act, namely pushing a man to steal his backpack, and the sanction: three years spent in jail, alternating crammed dormitories and solitary confinement, being submitted to guard discretion and gang violence.[7] A last objection must be discarded. After all, this case might simply be a judicial error and the judge might be the sole person responsible for it. Such an interpretation would thus exonerate the penal system. But actually no mistake was committed, and the whole legal procedure was perfectly respected and sadly banal. The young man's tragic story does not result from a dysfunction in the justice system of the United States; on the contrary, it attests to its ordinary functioning.

In sum, it is not a crime or even the suspicion of a crime that led to Browder's incarceration; his social properties, including his skin color, made him the usual suspect, and his mother's meager resources prevented the payment of the bail. Besides, the remand cannot be regarded as a mere administrative preventive measure; under the present circumstances, it appears to be a disguised sanction, which exceeds both in quantity, for the time spent imprisoned, and quality, for the conditions of the stay, the seriousness of the act of which he is accused. It is therefore legitimate to question the causal link and the relation of proportionality between the crime and the punishment, the former not being established and the latter having never been formulated as such.

The parallel between the two stories—which I take as a heuristic rather than systematic comparison—suggests a few preliminary conclusions. First, crime does not inevitably require punishment; alternate responses exist even for the most reprehensible offenses, including disregard. Second, punishment does not necessarily result from a crime; it can proceed from other logics not directly related to guilt, such as social or economic rationales, for instance. Third, a major crime can lead to a minor penalty and a minor offense to a major punishment; such discrepancy refutes the principle of adequacy of the retribution. Fourth, the actual punishment of an alleged crime may substantially exceed its apparent delimitation; the official sanction allows for much more redoubtable and invisible ones, independent of the seriousness of the alleged offense. To these four assertions a fifth could be added, which underlies the others. As can be seen in the two cases, the very notions of crime and punishment are not objects of consensus. They can be discussed and even disputed within both the social world and the intellectual realm. (What is a transgression that is not sanctioned? What is a measure that is viewed as punitive only by those who endure it? Who decides what is a crime and what is a punishment?) Instead of deciding on these matters, I consider it more judicious to try to understand what is at stake in these disagreements and contentions, preferring an ex post analysis to an a priori definition.

But the confrontation of the two narratives—for the contrasts they emphasize—also calls for a reflection of a distinct nature, focusing on the moral and political foundations of the concerned societies. Thus Trobriand Islanders seem to be flexible in the application of rules and lenient in the sanction of their violations, preferring gossip and rituals to retribution and, as a last resort, honor suicide to the infliction of suffering; they privilege accommodation over punishment as a mode of regulation of crime and deviance. By contrast, in the United States one favors repression over prevention, confines the alleged offenders, coerces the innocent to plead guilty, penalizes the poor more than the wealthy, and condones arbitrariness and violence at the heart of the penal system; social disorders are governed at the cost of inequity in the implementation of the law and unfairness in the distribution of sanctions. The point is not to establish moral hierarchies between societies but to reflect upon the diversity of possible political responses to the transgression of their norms. Being a social institution, punishment is indeed a remarkable social analyzer of the emotions elicited by crime and of the values mobilized in return.

What is punishment? Why does one punish? Who gets punished? These are the three questions I will try to answer. In other words, I will revisit the definition, justification, and distribution of punishment. These three questions will call for three others. *What is punishment?* invites us to wonder *whence* the idea of punishment comes. *Why does one punish?* extends into an interrogation on *how* one punishes. *Who gets punished?* appears to be inseparable from the exploration of *what* one chooses to punish. Needless to say, the scope of the inquiry is vast.

I will, however, set one limit to my analysis by restricting it to the public institutions in charge of deciding and applying punishment in matters of crime, notably politicians, legislators, the police, judges, and the corrections personnel, therefore excluding institutions operating in private spaces, such as the family, and institutions whose prime function is not punitive, such as the school and the workplace. It would certainly be interesting to study how

Western societies have come to condemn with increasing severity physical punishment inflicted on children by their parents and their teachers at the same time as they frantically developed the most punitive systems involving extreme bodily constraints, starting with the carceral institution, and to comprehend how the state has thus relentlessly expanded its monopoly of legitimate violence, but such an analysis would exceed the frame that I have decided to give to the current inquiry.

Even with this delimitation I have chosen to explore a territory much broader than is customary in studies on punishment. In the introduction of *Punishment and Modern Society*, David Garland characterizes his object in the following way: "Punishment is taken here to be the legal process whereby violators of the criminal law are condemned and sanctioned in accordance with specified legal categories and procedures."[8] While I consider this approach, which consists in defining one's object a priori in a Durkheimian manner, perfectly sound, I will proceed in a reverse, somewhat Weberian fashion, inductively striving to make a critical theory emerge from the empirical material I gathered—mine and that of others. Not presuming what punishment is, and even not presuming that it be the only possible response to crime, I allow myself to open other perspectives.

The three questions I address mark out paths that have been followed for more than two thousand years, first by philosophers, then by legal scholars, and more recently by political scientists, economists, sociologists, psychologists, historians, and anthropologists. To venture there is consequently not without risk of redundancy. In an attempt to avoid repetition, I will take less frequented side trails. Indeed the approach I propose is not conventional, as it escapes disciplinary delimitations. Hybrid, it borrows its tools from various kits that are not often mobilized together but that I found helpful to think conjointly. If a qualification was needed for this approach, one could call it a critical anthropology. As I envisage it, anthropology can be described as a way of apprehending social worlds with a propensity for astonishment, that is, a cultivated aptitude to consider any fact or situation not as the effect of a necessity but as the product of a certain social configuration inscribed in its time, which, had it been different, would have generated a distinct reality and is therefore destined to change. This awareness of the contingency of things that we usually take for granted—what an offense is and that it should be punished, for instance—does not have only an intellectual interest; it also has important moral and political implications.

The critical epistemology underlying this approach associates two complementary methods: genealogical and ethnographic. The genealogical method explores both the origins and the developments of contemporary conceptions about crime and punishment. To implement it, I will resort to philology, ethnology, and history so as to identify, in lexical corpuses, remote cultures and past worlds, traces allowing us to reconstitute how we have come to punish in the way we do it today. More than the genealogy of the relatively short time span generally used by Michel Foucault, I will privilege a genealogy in the longue durée as Nietzsche imagined it, being conscious of its pitfalls but confident in its heuristic potentiality to operate a radical rupture with self-evidence.[9] Indeed it is a matter of questioning what we think we know about what is punishment and why and whom we punish by proposing hypotheses that only the genealogical method allows. The ethnographic method relies on a long-term presence in a given social world, enabling the building of relationships of mutual trust with its members and the acquisition of a certain familiarity with their modes of thinking and acting. In particular I will refer to research I have conducted in the past ten years on law enforcement, the justice system, and the prison system in France. The first study focused on the largest police district in the country, where for fifteen months I accompanied police patrols, especially that of anticrime squads, in disadvantaged neighborhoods; the two most important recent urban disorders took place during that period. The second study concerned a short-stay correctional facility, where I was given full access to wards and cells day and night over a period of four years; I could thus attend disciplinary boards and parole commissions, meet freely with guards and inmates, directors and chaplains, magistrates and social workers, and sometimes even follow the penal career of offenders from their trial to their incarceration and finally liberation. The third study, more limited, consisted in the observation of approximately thirty immediate appearance hearings in the regional court, where most criminal cases were judged. These local research works were inscribed in a broader analysis, both sociological and political, of the repressive policies and practices of the French state.[10] Of this long-term research I have kept here only a few ethnographic moments deemed significant inasmuch as they question our common sense regarding the definition, the justification, and the distribution of punishment; the thick description of these studies has been presented elsewhere.

The two methods somewhat complement each other and participate in a common critical approach. Genealogy questions the foundations of punitive institutions. Ethnography uncovers its most concrete stakes. The former reveals the conditions of emergence for a specific configuration of the link between crime and punishment, of which the latter inquires what it enables or excludes, what it augments or diminishes, what it renders visible or makes disappear. To combine genealogy and ethnography in this way allows challenging classical approaches, both in philosophy and law, which have logically dominated modern and contemporary conceptions of crime and punishment and largely contributed to circumscribe the domain of the thinkable and the possible. The sort of disorientation that this method invites aims in particular at producing questions on the theoretical foundations of their assumptions and on the empirical discrepancy between their normative statements and the observed practices. The point is not that moral philosophers and legal scholars would all share the same doxa or partake in a homogeneous corpus. On the contrary, I will try to account for the diversity of their theses and the richness of their debates, with some of their critical approaches converging with my own analyses. But the social sciences can make other voices be heard and other realities be acknowledged—whether in the past, present, or future. It is therefore this critical dialogue that I hope to engage with disciplines that have with time constituted the major part of the current knowledge and practices regarding the act of punishing.

But the issue of punishment is not only a matter of academic discussion; it also presents a character of urgency as the world is undergoing an unprecedented punitive moment. Over the past half century, the prison population has multiplied by eight in the United States and by two and a half in France. Only during the 1990s it tripled in the Czech Republic, doubled in Italy and the Netherlands, increased by one-half in Britain, Portugal, Greece, Poland, Slovakia, Serbia, and Russia, and expanded by one-third in Germany, Belgium, Spain, Slovenia, and Croatia; exceptions to this European trend are found mostly in Scandinavian countries. At a global level, since 2000 the progression has been 107 percent in the Americas, excluding the United States, 29 percent in Asia, 15 percent in Africa, and 59 percent in Oceania. Of course the penal demography is only one indicator of the repressive turn of recent decades, and one would often have even more significant features by taking into account statistics of people under the supervision of correctional systems.[11] Remarkably this evolution is often not correlated to an upsurge in criminal activities. A complex phenomenon, it is mostly the consequence of a cultural change in the sensibilities and sensitivities to disorders and deviances and of a political instrumentalization of popular anxieties and hostilities; this penal populism, as it is often called, is itself underlain by profound socioeconomic transformations with growing inequalities within societies.[12] In this context, inquiring into the contemporary will to punish has become a democratic exigency.

Notes

1. Bronislaw Malinowski, "Primitive Crime and Its Punishment," in *Crime and Custom in Savage Society* (New York: Harcourt, Brace, 1926), 77–81.

2. Jennifer Gonnerman, "Before the Law," *New Yorker*, October 6, 2014, 26–32.

3. David Schneider, "Political Organization, Supernatural Sanctions and the Punishment of Incest on Yap," *American Anthropologist* 59 (1957): 791–800, esp. 791–92.

4. Keith Otterbein, *The Ultimate Coercive Sanction: A Cross-Cultural Study of Capital Punishment* (New Haven: HRAF Press, 1986), 24–25, 107.

5. Pheny Smith, *Felony Defendants in Large Urban Counties, 1990* (Washington, DC: U.S. Department of Justice, 1993); Brian Reaves, *Felony Defendants in Large Urban Counties, 2009* (Washington, DC: U.S. Department of Justice, 2013).

6. Jed Rakoff, "Why Innocent People Plead Guilty," *New York Review of Books*, November 20, 2014.

7. U.S. Attorney, Southern District of New York, *Civil Rights of Institutionalized Persons Act: Investigation of the New York City Department of Correction Jails on Rikers Island* (New York: U.S. Department of Justice, 2014).

8. David Garland, *Punishment and Modern Society: A Study in Social Theory* (Chicago: University of Chicago Press, 1990), 17.

9. Michel Foucault, "What Is Enlightenment?," in *The Foucault Reader*, ed. Paul Rabinow. (New York: Pantheon Books, 1984), 32–50; Friedrich Nietzsche, *On the Genealogy of Morals*, trans. Walter Kaufman (New York: Vintage Books, 1989), first published in German in 1887.

10. Didier Fassin, *Enforcing Order: An Ethnography of Urban Policing*, trans. Rachel Gomme (Cambridge, UK: Polity Press, 2013), first published in French in 2011; Didier Fassin, *Prison Worlds: An Ethnography of the Carceral Condition*, trans. Rachel Gomme (Cambridge, UK: Polity Press, 2016), first published in French in 2015. The cases drawn from my fieldwork and presented here can be found with more detail in these two books.

11. Institute for Criminal Policy Research, "World Prison Brief," http://www.prisonstudies.org/about-wpb; Roy Walmsley, "Global Incarceration and Prison Trends," *Forum on Crime and Society* 3.1–2 (2003): 65–78.

12. Julian Roberts, Loretta Stalans, David Indermaur, and Mike Hough, *Penal Populism and Public Opinion: Lessons from Five Countries* (Oxford: Oxford University Press, 2003); John Pratt, *Penal Populism* (London: Routledge, 2007).

Chapter 1: What Is Punishment?

For the past fifty years, most writings on punishment have referred to the definition provided by the British legal philosopher H. L. A. Hart in his presidential address before the Aristotelian Society in 1959.[1] Writing in the context of a heated and confused debate on the death penalty at the House of Lords, the Oxford academic insisted on the importance of clarifying what punishment is before asking what justifies it. According to what he called "the standard or central case," five elements were necessary to characterize punishment in criminal matters: it must "involve pain or other consequences normally considered unpleasant; be for an offense against legal rules; be of an actual or supposed offender for his offense; be intentionally administered by human beings other than the offender; be imposed and administered by an authority constituted by a legal system against which the offense is committed." These five criteria state not only what punishment is but also, by subtraction, what it is not. While seemingly offering a pure description of it, they legitimize it on two grounds: moral, since it concerns an offense and applies to the offender; legal, since it is how the rule that has been infringed and the authority that decides and executes the sanction are described.

Thus, although Hart insists on the necessity of distinguishing definition and justification, his characterization of punishment amounts to justifying it and even more to justifying its core modality: the infliction of a pain or softer equivalent to the person who has committed a reprehensible act. Of the authority of his definition and its potential consequences, he is himself perfectly conscious. He even acknowledges that there exist other forms of punishment—vicarious, affecting people for the action of one of them, or extralegal, for breaches of rules that are not inscribed in the law—and it is evident that if these other forms were taken into account, they would weaken the moral legitimacy of the sanction in the first case and its legal legitimacy in the second. He designates them, however, as "sub-standard or secondary cases" and does not envisage them further.

One should therefore wonder what one loses and what one eclipses by accepting Hart's standard definition.[2] In the following pages I will, first, starting with an ethnographic observation, discuss the relevance of the five criteria, showing that only one resists this empirical test, and second, resorting to a genealogical analysis, investigate how this criterion has come to define what punishing means.

Let us consider an incident that occurred during my fieldwork with law enforcement patrols a few months before the 2005 riots in France. One late afternoon the resident of a small housing project calls the police to inform them on the presence of a noisy quad bike in the park nearby. A crew is quickly dispatched to the site, and on their arrival the three officers attempt to intercept the vehicle. Trying to escape, the young driver falls off his vehicle without hurting himself, and the officers rush to catch him. As they are bringing him under control, several youths come to the defense of their friend, surrounding the police and protesting the arrest. Feeling threatened, the three officers decide to retreat and call the precinct for reinforcements. A few minutes later half a dozen vehicles, including unmarked ones with anticrime squads on board, arrive at the scene with lights flashing and sirens wailing. More than a dozen officers storm into the park, where families are still enjoying the long spring daylight with children playing near their parents. As they try to catch at random the youths hanging around, officers run into some of these peaceful bystanders, stirring up protests. A woman who loudly interposes herself to protect her son is forcibly apprehended. A nine-year-old boy who has talked back to an officer is menaced with a Flash-Ball next to his face. Convinced that they have identified the leader of the group initially involved—a young man of African origin known to be active in local drug trafficking—the police hustle into the staircase of the three-story building and break the door of the apartment where his parents live. Aggressively searching for the youth, they knock over his sister as she comes out of her bedroom having heard the turmoil. They finally find the suspect, pin him down, handcuff him, and take him in for questioning, only to discover that he is blind, which makes him the very unlikely perpetrator of an assault; they eventually release him. Of the dozen residents, mostly youths, who have been taken in for questioning, five, including the rebellious mother, are held in custody under the charge of insulting the police and resisting arrest, while the others are freed and left outside the precinct in the middle of the night with almost three miles to walk back home. Hospitalized, the blind man's sister is diagnosed with a broken arm and a neck lesion.

The scene I just described is not uncommon in disadvantaged French neighborhoods. During my research I have witnessed or heard of several similar episodes, more or less serious, and, when they go wrong, it is this sort of incident that can provoke the death of a resident and lead to urban disorders. Fortunately most of them have less harmful conclusions and are ignored by the public, except those who are directly affected. But how to interpret the reaction of law enforcement agents to what three of their colleagues had considered a hindrance to their intervention? How to qualify this brutal expedition that leaves material damage as well as physical injuries among the inhabitants and ends up with unconvincing apprehensions? In view of Hart's definition, one is tempted to refute an interpretation in terms of punishment. Indeed the pain endured and distress experienced as well as the intention to cause them cannot be denied, but one may wonder whether the arrests are related to any offense, whether those arrested are at all offenders, and ultimately whether it is in the legal mission of the police to punish. In fact the residents do not hesitate to say that these are reprisals, and some, among them law enforcement officials, hint at the same analysis.

Punishment or vengeance? Philosophers have long tried to oppose them, judging the latter wrong and illegitimate, the former right and legitimate. In his *Summa Theologica,* speaking only of vengeance, as is common in the Christian doctrine of his time, Thomas Aquinas considers that the difference between lawfulness and unlawfulness resides in the intention of the one who corrects the sin. If it is "directed chiefly to the evil of the person on whom he takes vengeance and rests there, then his vengeance is unlawful: because to take pleasure in another's evil belongs to hatred." However, if it is "directed chiefly to some good to be obtained by means of the punishment of the person who has sinned, then vengeance may be lawful" as it is intended to amend the sinner or avoid his committing more sins.[3] Many philosophers have since then attempted to characterize the difference between punishment and vengeance. In an often cited text, while admitting that "retribution and revenge share a common structure: a penalty is inflicted for a reason (a wrong or an injury) with the desire that the other person know why this is occurring and know that he was intended to know," Robert Nozick proposes five criteria to distinguish them. Retribution is "done for a wrong"; it "sets an internal limit to the amount of the punishment, according to the seriousness of the wrong"; it implies "no special or personal tie to the victim of the wrong"; it involves "pleasure at justice being done"; it is "committed to general principles mandating punishment in other similar circumstances." Conversely, revenge "may be done for an injury or harm or slight and need not be done for a wrong"; it "need set no limits"; it "is personal"; it involves an "emotional tone"; it has "no generality."[4] The distinction has not only an explicit moral objective of delegitimizing revenge in order to better legitimize retribution, but also an implicit political goal of separating "the others" (the barbarians who avenge) from "our people" (the civilized who punish), a division that resonates with the contemporary context wherein Western societies have become more repressive while being increasingly confronted by new forms of violence emanating from other parts of the world.

But is it so easy to distinguish the two? "Does Othello punish Desdemona or does he take revenge upon her for what he thought was her betrayal? Is the Count of Monte Cristo punishing or taking revenge on the malefactors who attempted to ruin his life?" asks Leo Zaibert, for whom this distinction is in fact more rhetorical than analytical.[5] It is an analogous question that Danielle Allen poses concerning the suffering inflicted by Zeus on Prometheus in Aeschylus's tragedy: "We are not certain whether it is an act of punishment or an act of torture," as the god affirms that it is just retribution for the theft of fire while the titan claims that it is mere cruel revenge.[6] If, rather than in the literature, we take illustrations in the real world to test Nozick's criteria that supposedly discriminate the two notions, can we consider that the death penalty inflicted for a homicide corresponds only to a wrong and not to an injury, that the amputation of the thief's hand is proportionate to the seriousness of the offense, that the whipping of a slave accused of having robbed his master proceeds from impersonal arbitration, that the public execution of a convict is exempt of emotional tone, and finally that the hanging of a tyrant after the fall of his regime follows general principles of justice? Yet in each of these examples, most people agree, including the judges officially in charge of deciding the sentences, that such acts correspond to retribution and not revenge. This difficulty of separating one from the other was recognized by Émile Durkheim, for whom "punishment has remained for us what it was for our predecessors: it is still an act of vengeance since it is an expiation."[7] In his view, however, revenge does not have the negative connotation that moralists attach to it, but is the beneficial expression of a sort of self-defense.

Returning to the intervention of the police in the housing project, we cannot simply see it as an operation to maintain public order, in consideration of the disorder that it actually provokes, or to defend public security, in light of the insecurity that it evidently generates. But can we be satisfied with the qualification of reprisal, which would amount to exonerating the institution by reducing the brutal expedition to mere inappropriate individual reactions? I contend that this scene should rather be interpreted as a punitive operation. To demonstrate it, I will rely on subjective (the officers' perception) as well as objective (the observer's analysis) elements.

The officers themselves would never depict their action as reprisal. They could obviously not claim it as such in front of their superiors or judges, since they are not supposed to exert vengeance on the population they should be serving. But their private conversations show that it is not the way they see things either: they even develop arguments to legitimize this type of operation. Their justifications are mostly of two kinds. First, they regard the residents of disadvantaged neighborhoods as hostile, a representation that enables their own hostility in return. "They don't like us, and we don't like them either," the head of the anticrime squad liked to say. Besides, they systematically associate them with crime, especially the youths, and admit that they have a hard time distinguishing "thugs from honest people," in the words of the commissioner. This negative image, which proceeds by generalizing certain traits to the whole population, is often underlain by racist and xenophobic prejudices against people of color or immigrant background. Thus, viewing their public as composed of probable enemies and potential criminals, despite the evidence of the opposite from opinion polls and field observations, the officers feel entitled to punish them with little discernment. Second, they deem the justice system ineffective and the magistrates too lenient. "We arrest criminals and indict them, but the next day they are back in the street" is a litany among rank-and-file agents. Although statistics demonstrate, on the contrary, that the penal institution is increasingly severe, this belief justifies various forms of immediate retribution, from bullying to beating up. Even if the arrested suspect is later freed, he will have had a hard time, they think, and some justice will have been dispensed in the street or at the precinct. From their perspective, this unofficial punishment anticipates and corrects the supposed clemency of the judges.

The observer, for his part, can expand the local scene by relating it to its historical and political context. Indeed this police operation is not an isolated fact; it is part of the habitual and expected modes of law enforcement interventions in disadvantaged neighborhoods.[8] Of the anticrime squads, a commissioner told me that they were "a necessary evil," and a high official commented that they were "the darlings of their superiors" because they bring arrests. From the police academy, where the training of future officers mostly from rural areas and small towns consolidates their prejudices concerning the housing projects and their inhabitants, to the disciplinary boards, where impunity for deviant behaviors is the rule, the institution contributes to the permanence of targeted punitive practices and the legitimization of their justifications. Such practices are moreover encouraged by the public discourse of law and order, the insistent stigmatization of certain populations, the imposition of unattainable quotas of arrests, and finally national policies that provide the police their technological as well as legal instruments and guarantee them protection in case of misconduct or incident. A former French minister of the interior, who was later elected president, is remembered for saying about housing projects that he would "clean them out with a Kärcher" and about their youths that he would "get rid of this scum." In this context the police are quasi-officially empowered with such forms of extrajudiciary punishment.

In view of the subjective and objective elements gathered to interpret the intervention of the police, one can therefore reasonably argue that it is a punitive operation. This interpretation has two important theoretical implications. First, rather than attempting to verify that facts match the definition, one should strive to adapt the latter to the former: the meaning that agents give to their acts and the analysis one can make of what underlies them lead here to contest the proposed criteria. Second, while it is conceptually legitimate to try to separate definition from justification, as many scholars do, it is empirically difficult and perhaps politically problematic to do so; officers and their institution do need arguments, albeit fallacious, to legitimize what would otherwise appear as deviance.

If we accept this reading of the scene in the housing project, what sort of retribution is involved, since the actual offenders—whether we consider the driver of the quad or the youths who came to his rescue—were not arrested? Two possible modes may be distinguished: collective and random. Collective punishment consists in sanctioning the whole group to which the alleged culprit belongs, namely the residents, more specifically the teenagers, who are present in the public place. Their tranquility is upset; their environment is disrupted; some are insulted and menaced, while others are pushed around or knocked over. They learn the hard way that whatever their age, sex, and status, they may at any time find themselves at the mercy of the police, for no reason and without possible recourse. Random punishment entails penalizing those, within the group, who can make plausible suspects, either because of their criminal record or simply because they are at hand. They are searched, sometimes arrested, and even indicted. A crucial element in this process is the fabrication of the offense of insulting the police and resisting arrest, with which those who have been particularly mistreated will be charged, their injuries being presented to the judge as the consequences of bringing them under control. The punishment in the street is thus doubled with a sentence in court. Although their superiors regard these practices as indicative of the aggressiveness of the agents more than of the violence of their public, the police have been encouraged by the Ministry of the Interior to charge liberally with this offense, the result being a boom in the corresponding sentences during the past three decades.

Putting together the various pieces of the puzzle in light of the classical definition of punishment, we can see that the police operation is conducted by a legal institution that is not designed to punish but considers itself entitled and is incited by public authorities to do so; that the offenses sanctioned do not match the initial motive of the intervention and can even be fabricated so as to neutralize potential complaints; that in the absence of an identifiable offender, the sanction can translate into punitive expedition or random punishment; and that it adopts extralegal forms such as physical and moral abuse.

What has just been described for France is in no way specific. In recent years law enforcement agencies have increasingly appeared, in various parts of the globe, as suppliers of extrajudicial punishment. In Brazil human rights organizations calculated that more than five thousand people were killed by the police between 2005 and 2014 in Rio de Janeiro as part of the so-called pacification of the favelas. In the Philippines official statistics reveal that during the sole months of July and August 2016 more than eighteen hundred suspects were shot dead, including seven hundred by the police, as a result of the war on drugs declared by the newly elected president. In the United States 1,134 deaths caused by the police were registered in 2015, that is, forty times more than those by capital punishment during the same period, and remarkably, the socioracial profile of victims is similar.[9] The interpretation of these homicides as extrajudiciary punishments varies according to the context: in some cases the statements made by politicians and the positive reactions from part of the population leave no doubt about a well-assumed penal populism; in others, the support of these practices by the authorities, their facilitation by the institution, the impunity they benefit from, and the complacent silence that accompanies them indicate latent or veiled expressions of this populism. But the punitive function of law enforcement should not be reduced to these extreme manifestations. On a daily basis, for many belonging to the most vulnerable groups, it translates into harassment, provocations, humiliations, racist insults, undue stops, unjustified searches, abusive fines, painful handcuffing, groundless arrests, arbitrary custody, blows leaving no trace, sometimes even torture.[10] The trivialization and normalization of extrajudiciary punishment by the police represent a major unrecognized fact of contemporary societies.

In an influential essay that inspired Hart's definition, Antony Flew suggests that "there is no sharp line drawn at which we must stop" in the very use of the word: "When does punishment of the innocent or illegal punishment cease to be properly called punishment at all?"[11] The question is legitimate, and in the case just presented the two elements of innocence and illegality are combined. But precisely on the basis of these observations, we could reverse the reasoning and rather wonder whether it is not the definition of the word that should be revised in light of the facts it is supposed to describe. Are the punishment of the innocent and the illegal punishment not ordinary forms of retribution? Would the purification of the act of punishing from what would not be legal or legitimate, whereas everything indicates that societies have never ceased to punish beyond the principles ordered by law and morality, not amount to substituting the ideality of the phenomenon for its reality, thus conjuring away the latter? This is not a matter of cynicism but the condition for a sound depiction of what is rather than what ought to be. Revisiting the five criteria then becomes a heuristic as well as a political necessity.

The second and third criteria of Hart's definition seem prima facie the most obvious: punishment applies when a (legal) rule has been violated and concerns the person who has committed (or is suspected to have committed) this transgression. In the case discussed, we have seen, however, that these two principles may not be respected: we have random punishment and forged offenses. If these are common practices among the police, they can also be found within other institutions, starting with schools, where collective sanctions are not uncommon when the guilty student does not denounce himself or is not denounced by others. But it is in the context of international conflicts that they take the most tragic turn, as numerous episodes of the two world wars have shown. For the contemporary period, the Israeli government is regularly condemned by international organizations for its systematic use of collective retribution against Palestinians: demolition of the houses of attackers' families; revocation of travel permits for tens of thousands of people after assaults; spraying of putrid water on homes and schools in neighborhoods where protests have taken place; bombing of civilians, such as during the operation known as Protective Edge, which caused more than two thousand deaths, including those of numerous children and women.[12] Although these punitive actions may be designated as reprisals by the United Nations and denounced as such by human rights organizations, including in Israel, they are always presented by the Israeli government as legitimate punishment in terms of both just deserts and effective deterrence, that is, in the very language of law.[13] Such disputes are a reminder that deciding what punishment is always involves both moral and political stakes.

The penal system itself contributes to blurring the borders of the punitive domain, as shown by the demographics of prisons. If one takes seriously the assertion according to which a person accused of a crime is innocent until proven guilty, one must admit that those awaiting trial should not receive an anticipated punishment by being imprisoned. Yet in the United States, of the twelve million people sent to jail each year, 62 percent are not convicted and 75 percent have been accused of nonviolent offenses. In France people on remand represent 29 percent of the total number of inmates but 43 percent of those in short-stay facilities.[14] Although this is not considered a punishment but a preventive measure to avoid other offenses and ensure their presence at the trial, a warden commented to me that, paradoxically, those under this procedure are detained in harsher conditions than the convicts: they are confined much longer during the day in overcrowded cells; they have less access to work and education; their prerogatives within the facility are more restricted; in the end it may not be fortuitous that their suicide rate is almost three times higher than for the average carceral population. But there exist other forms of dissociation between crime and punishment, the most extreme probably being the denial of retrial for innocent persons wrongly convicted and the institution of indefinite detention without trial. In the first instance, of which various examples have been reported in the United States, judges reject on specious arguments the reopening of cases after the finding of new evidence establishing the innocence of individuals incarcerated or even facing execution.[15] In the second instance, governments institute legal dispositions allowing individuals to be detained for an unlimited time without being convicted or even indicted, as is the case for undocumented migrants or asylum seekers in Britain and Australia and for political prisoners or so-called enemy combatants in Guantanamo and Israel.[16] In these cases, the absence of crime does not suffice to guarantee the absence of punishment.

The fourth and fifth criteria of Hart's definition concern the administration of the punishment, namely the persons who execute it and the authority that imposes it. On the one hand, punishment is supposed to be inflicted by someone other than the offender. Yet what do we know about the meaning of the suicide or self-mutilation of someone convicted and, most of the time, incarcerated? The interpretation of the harm he does to himself can be quite delicate: is it to call for help, to protest against an intolerable situation, to escape the prospect of torture, or strictly speaking to mortify himself for the crime committed? The topic is particularly sensitive in France, which has the highest prison suicide rate in Europe. However, the fact that perpetrators of homicide kill themselves three times more often than the general population of inmates suggests that guilt plays a significant role in their act, which can then be assimilated to a self-inflicted punishment.[17] On the other hand, punishment is expected to be dispensed by a legal authority. But whereas the state typically exercises the monopoly of the use of legitimate violence, it actually faces the presence of other actors who also claim a right to mete out justice or more exactly to take the law into their own hands. The most significant phenomenon in that regard is the development of what is called, after a Spanish word, vigilantism. It covers disparate kinds of mobilizations, from the Ku Klux Klan in the South of the United States not long ago to the Minutemen at the Mexican border today, from El Salvador's Sombra Negra to South Africa's People against Gangsterism and Drugs. Beyond their differences both ideological and tactical, these movements of citizens have in common that they deem the official authorities incapable of solving security issues and they commit themselves to replace the official authorities by punishing the suspects they arrest. If these self-defense groups are outlaws, they often have ambiguous relationships with the state, particularly with its police.[18] It is consequently difficult to consider that punishment is necessarily administered by someone else than the criminal and under a recognized legal authority.

One criterion ultimately remains of the initial definition: the infliction of pain—or, at least, of some form of unpleasantness. This is also what is retained by common sense and clearly expressed by Durkheim: "It is claimed that we do not make the guilty person suffer for the sake of suffering. It is nevertheless true that we deem it fair that he should suffer."[19] In effect, the semantic equivalence between punishment and suffering goes together with the penal equivalence between crime and suffering: it is because to punish is to inflict suffering that philosophers, jurists, legislators, magistrates have applied themselves to establish a minutely detailed correspondence between the offense committed and the misery inflicted, and conversely, it is because one estimates that the atonement for the act necessitates a certain quantum of pain that to punish must mean to make suffer.

This circular reasoning seems so self-evident that its equivalences are not contested any more. Yet in his address, Hart strongly warned against the risk of taking them for granted.[20] Inviting his audience not to restrain themselves to his "standard case," he insisted on the danger of a "definitional stop" that "would prevent us from investigating the very thing which modern skepticism most calls into question: namely the rational and moral status of our preference for a system of punishment under which measures painful to individuals are to be taken against them only when they have committed an offense." To confine ourselves to a definition associating punishment with suffering would be to renounce any foundational critique by eluding the interrogation: "Why do we prefer this to other forms of social hygiene which we might employ instead to prevent anti-social behavior?" To avoid this pitfall, we must therefore complement the question: What is punishment? by this other: Whence does our idea of a punishment come?

In the second essay of the *Genealogy of Morals,* Nietzsche was probably the first author to dispute the self-evidence of punishment as infliction of pain.[21] "Whence did this primeval, deeply rooted, perhaps by now ineradicable idea draw its power—this idea of an equivalence between injury and pain?" he asks. And his answer cannot fail to surprise: it comes from "the contractual relationship between creditor and debtor, which is as old as the idea of legal subjects, and in turn points back to the fundamental forms of buying, selling, barter, trade and traffic." The linguistic link seems clear in German as "the major moral concept *Schuld* [guilt] has its origin in the very material concept *Schulden* [debts]." But how and why was this original relationship established? "To inspire trust in his promise to repay, to provide a guarantee of the seriousness and sanctity of his promise, to impress repayment as a duty, an obligation upon his own conscience, the debtor made a contract with the creditor and pledged that if he should fail to repay he would substitute something else that he 'possessed,' something he had control over; for example, his body, his wife, his freedom, or even his life," while for his part, "the creditor could inflict every kind of indignity and torture upon the body of the debtor, for example cut from it as much as seemed commensurate with the size of the debt." A singular restitution system indeed.

When reading these lines, one may think of Shylock, the Jewish usurer of *The Merchant of Venice* who agrees to lend money to a young nobleman only on condition that, if the sum is not repaid by a certain date, his loan's guarantor, Antonio, who is the lender's rival in business, commits himself to have "a pound of flesh" taken from his own body.[22] As the debtor cannot pay on time, his creditor decides to exact revenge, recalling the insults, injuries, and humiliations he has endured from him and concluding his famous monologue with the verse "If you wrong us, do we not revenge?" In the play the repayment of the debt becomes the vengeance of a tort. This is precisely what Nietzsche questions: Why does the punishment of insolvency imply the infliction of pain? Why even establish an equivalence between the two? In broadening this enlightening intuition, I propose bringing a triple series of converging empirical elements about the genealogical link between debt and punishment: philological, ethnological, and historical.

The terms *punish* and *punishment* come from Old French *punir* and *punissement*, which have their origin in Medieval Latin *punire* or *pœnire*, "to chastise" or "to avenge," and, further back in time, Classical Latin *poena*, itself derived from Greek *poinē* (*ποινη*). In his study of Indo-European languages, Émile Benveniste discusses the last term under three entries, including that on "gift and exchange," and uses examples from *The Iliad*.[23] The notion refers to "the debt which must be paid to atone for a crime," "the retribution that compensates a murder," "the reparation due for violation of an oath." It means "to cause to pay a premium," "to claim the price of a fine, especially for a capital offense," while "also developed the emotional sense of hate, of vengeance." It is also the signification of exchange that is found in Classical Latin *poena*, which means "ransom to redeem a murder," as early as in the enactment of the Twelve Tables; hence "compensation, reparation, vengeance, punishment, chastisement." Only in Late Latin does the association with "torment" and "suffering" appear.[24] Until now French *peine* maintains the ambiguity of punishment and suffering, while the English distinguishes pain from penalty.

A somewhat parallel evolution can be identified for the word *retribution*, which comes from Latin *retributio* and *retribuere*. The latter verb is composed of the prefix *re-*, "in return," and *tribuere*, literally "to divide among tribes." It means "to give in exchange," "to pay in return," "to restitute what is owed" in the dual sense of recompense and punishing.[25] While the word is initially neutral, meaning either reward or reprisal, depending on whether the concerned deed was good or evil, it takes a moral orientation in the sixteenth century, conspicuously adopting opposite directions in French and English: essentially positive in the first case, mostly negative in the second. In the religious language of the time, *rétribution* refers to the fair salary rewarding the merit, under the Calvinist influence, while retribution evokes the Last Judgment and God's Wrath, from a literal reading of the Bible. In any case, *rétribution* currently means what is earned from work and, in a theological context, recompense, whereas retribution mainly evokes the idea of punishment for a wrong or an injury, and in philosophical texts, a theory of just deserts.

This modest linguistic exercise suggests a remarkable semantic development. Originally the terms from which the vocabulary of punishment derives designated a restitution in relation to a debt: the reparation of a crime (*pœna*), a repayment as obligation or gratification (*retribuere*). The semantic network in which these words were inscribed was that of exchange. They could have an affective connotation of anger or hatred, but not a moral meaning. The association with pain appears in the first century for *pœna*, and the two ideas of remuneration for *rétribution* and punishment for retribution emerge around the Renaissance. Suffering and morality thus combine to turn punishment into a torment inflicted for a sin. A new semantic network is constituted in the language of fault, guilt, and just deserts. Punishment used to entail a debt to repay; it has become a suffering to inflict.

Of this ancient economy of the debt, ethnology offers numerous examples. Thus about the Tlingit Indians of southeastern Alaska he studied in the early 1930s, Kalervo Oberg writes that "in the matter of crime and punishment" it was the clan rather than the individual that counted: "Theoretically, crime against an individual did not exist."[26] Since each clan was hierarchically structured, the imputation of crime to the clan meant that "if a man of low rank killed a man of high rank in another clan, the murderer often went free while one of his more important kinsmen suffered death in his stead," and conversely, "if the murdered man happened to be of low rank and of poor reputation, a payment of goods could satisfy the injured clan." A complex set of rules defining the treatment of the various offenses contributed to the manifestation and reproduction of the social order. This performative function of punishment relied on the dissociation between the offender and the penalty. It was inscribed in a process of circulation of persons and goods between clans rather than implying their individual responsibility. The violation of the moral norm or of the social order created a debt that the group had to repay—and not a fault that the individual had to expiate.

One can imagine that, for such societies, colonization may have sometimes given rise to a violent confrontation between the opposite rationales of exchange and suffering in the resolution of offenses. Having conducted research for three decades on the legal system of the Kapauku of Papua New Guinea, Leopold Pospisil analyzed the painful transition, starting in the 1950s, between the "primitive law" and the "civilized law," as he calls them, namely the set of rules and sanctions of Aborigines, on one side, and the judicial and repressive apparatus established by the Netherlands first and by Indonesia later, on the other.[27] In the system that prevailed before colonization, the Kapauku "regarded individual freedom as, possibly, their most valuable possession," which was deemed "a condition for life." It was therefore unthinkable to have one of them deprived of it when an offense was committed. Most of the time, paying for the damage done sufficed to compensate the violation of the rules, even in the case of a murder. Only when this obligation was not satisfied could physical punishment be envisaged. When the colonizers arrived, they introduced their penal system and carceral institutions. But for the Kapauku, imprisonment was inconceivable and intolerable, in complete contradiction with their philosophy of life. Bereft of what they most valued, prisoners let themselves die. The population, indignant at these inhumane practices, soon rebelled. The revolt was harshly repressed by the Dutch. Ten years later a new uprising led to a negotiated solution, this time with the Indonesian government. Such disturbances thus attest to the potential tensions between a justice system relying on the compensation of a debt through an exchange of goods and a justice system relying on the punishment of a wrong by the infliction of a pain.

Certain societies have combined both systems, however, and continue to do so. In Islamic law the resolution of a crime, as long as it has not been committed against God, can follow rationales of reparation or retribution. According to Qur'anic prescriptions, the punishment of a homicide can take two forms. *Qisas* corresponds to the principle of equal retaliation, an eye for an eye, the murder calling for the death of the murderer in return. *Diyya* offers the alternative of a financial compensation inasmuch as the relatives of the victim accept it. This is often known as "blood money," the amount of which is decided by the judge, depending in particular on the sex and religion of the victim. When the family of the perpetrator cannot afford the payment of a compensation, the Qur'an even recommends that the victim renounce the payment out of compassion and therefore forgive. This practice has been maintained or reinstated in countries with a majority of Muslims applying sharia law, but it can present various types of hybridization with Western criminal law. For instance, in the Islamic Republic of Iran the justice system regards intentional homicides as being both a private matter, for which the relatives of the victim can choose between vengeance and reparation, and a public case, in which the prosecutor may request a prison sentence.[28] Depending on national contexts, complex combinations thus develop between punishment and compensation.

As for the Western world, history reveals an ambiguous relationship between debt and penalty in Antiquity. In the opening lines of a pioneering article on debt bondage, Moses Finley recounts this mythological narrative: "In Delphi, the god told Heracles that the ailment from which he suffered was his punishment for the disloyal murder of Iphitos, and that he would be able to heal only by selling himself as a slave for a certain amount of time and by giving the sum thus obtained to the parents of the victim. This is how he was sold to Omphale, the queen of Lydia, and served his penalty working for her."[29] Here the crime is punished by the god who inflicts a pain on the murderer, but the atonement goes by way of reparation in the world of human beings: the salaries earned through bonded labor must allow the murderer to repay his debt to the bereaved family. There is thus a disconnection between the punishment (divine) and the compensation (human), the latter canceling the former. It is a matter of debt for which the god is only an intermediary. In "ancient and primitive societies," as the historian names them, such debts covered a wide spectrum of activities: they could come from "violent acts, such as a murder," as well as "gracious acts, such as a gift or any other favor." To use the simplest case, when loans of money or wheat were not restituted on time, compensation was imposed in the form of nonpaid work and occasionally even servitude for the borrower and his wife and children. Such was the meaning of the guarantee that the creditor included in the initial negotiation of the bond, as Nietzsche had noted. This debt bondage system, which had a considerable economic and demographic expansion, notably in Greece and Rome in the early times, allowed wealthy families to enjoy indefinitely a captive and gratuitous labor force.

In this particular case of debt bondage, two important elements should be retained from a genealogical perspective. On the one hand, crime belonged to an ensemble of legal and economic acts, either positively or negatively valued, including murder as well as loan, whose common feature was to create for certain individuals an obligation to other individuals. On the other hand, the social practices used to clear the debt thus incurred entailed the circulation and appropriation of goods and persons, servitude being their most extreme form. This does not mean that vengeance did not exist and that a murder never called for a murder in return. But in the case of the Roman Republic, for instance, such actions, in the absence of a criminal justice system, pertained to the private domain and, rather than moral judgments, implied emotional responses such as resentment.[30] They were, however, the exception, and most of the time the death of a person called for another way, more peaceful and more literal, to pay the price.

The question is therefore to understand how and perhaps why Western societies have undertaken this transition from a compensatory logic to a punitive logic, from an affective economy of debt to a moral economy of punishment. A compelling answer is offered by Georg Simmel in his *Philosophy of Money*.[31] Being interested in the monetary equivalence of human life in various cultures and times, he examines how murders were formerly sanctioned by a financial reparation known as *wergild* in contexts as distant as Anglo-Saxon England and Medieval Florence. In his view, two broad historical periods can be distinguished: in the first, the expiation of the crime operated as "the restitution of actual damage to the survivors calculated according to their status"; in the second, it became "punishment in the full sense of the term," that is, "a pain imposed by the idea of expediency." The passage from the former to the latter resulted from two facts: one political, the other sociological. On the one hand, the litigation generated by the crime committed was not settled between individuals any more, with the victim having the option of accepting financial reparation, but indirectly through the state or, more often, the Church, with the offense being deemed the violation of a general legal or moral principle and the atonement implying pain inflicted on the offender. On the other hand, the growing socioeconomic differentiation rendered the establishment of a just sanction increasingly problematic because it did not aim to compensate the damage any more but the crime itself, and because the corresponding suffering had to incorporate the fact that a wealthy individual might be hardly affected by the mere payment of a fine. The financial compensation thus became less and less relevant as the criminal act took a general meaning and its resolution shifted from the victim to the perpetrator.

It is a somewhat different approach that Michel Foucault adopts in his second series of lectures at the Collège de France.[32] Also focusing on the relationships between penal and political institutions in the Middle Ages, he devotes a significant part of his analysis to the transition from Germanic to Roman law and the power games that surround it. In Germanic law the settlement of litigation relied on compensation rather than revenge. Financial arrangements prevailed over physical chastisements, with the exception of rape, incest, and treason, which were punished by death or, more often, banishment. Even homicide had its codified scale of reparation through the payment of the wergild, the main function of which was to terminate the conflict: "It is the closure of the war, it is not the punishment of the wrong." With the Roman law, which imposed itself as the authority of the Church grew and the power of the king expanded, the practice of compensation was replaced by the discourse of redemption. From then on one spoke of faults and sins, calling for penalty and penitence. The notion of atonement did not concern material goods any more but spiritual ones, although the system of indulgences allowed resorting to both: "A description of penal practices in the Middle Ages should undoubtedly be ordered around the question: Who repays what; what does one repay such or such action for?" However, this transformation did not imply only "superstructures," that is, the juridical and the religious. It had above all fiscal and political implications, through the multiple types of fines, fees, confiscations, and acquisitions, which nourished the struggles between jurisdictions, favored the consolidation of the kingship, and enabled the enrichment of Catholic institutions: it was "very directly inscribed in the game of relations of appropriation and domination." In the end, the medieval penal system seemed to serve less to ensure the ideological control of the people via the morality of the fault and the theology of the sin than to facilitate the circulation of wealth and the concentration of powers.

Whereas, more Marxist than he would have liked to admit, Foucault interprets the profound transformations of the criminal law in the Middle Ages from the angle of a political economy of penal institutions, I consider for my part at least as important to comprehend them from the perspective of a moral economy of punishment—in other words, through the way in which values and affects are produced, disseminated, adopted, distorted, and contested around the responses imagined to confront crime. One therefore needs a resolutely longer temporality to seize the passage from the logic of debt, which has long prevailed, to the logic of wrong, as it progressively imposed itself in the Western world, mainly under the influence of Christianity. It is that of Nietzsche's genealogy. In the Middle Ages "the judge is seated under a crucifix," observes Valérie Toureille, adding that "he nevertheless believes in the rational use of justice."[33] In this shift from reparation to punishment, suffering occupies a crucial place. It atones the sins: suffering is imposed on the person who must also accept it. During the Classical Age, while public executions are as rare as they are harrowing for the torments inflicted, it is deemed important that "the convicts behave humbly on the scaffold, showing repentance," going as far as "to kneel down in front of the judges and express their gratitude," thus making the event a "beautiful execution," as Pieter Spierenburg explains.[34] The exaltation of suffering exceeds the desire of vengeance, especially since punishment is now mediated via the justice system. It is reflected in people's daily life and places of worship through the omnipresent representations of the Agony of the Christ, who dies on the cross to save humanity by redeeming original sin, as well as in the depictions of the torments of martyrs, who attest to their faith and the existence of God by their self-sacrifice. The conception of punishment as suffering is indeed inscribed within a soteriology in which only the infliction of pain can give access to redemption and salvation.

But the valuation of suffering exceeds the framework of punishment. In the Middle Ages notably, having committed a crime is not the only case in which one may experience affliction. Penitence, mortification, and even flagellation are part and parcel of Christian practices, especially among monks and nuns. Confinement is regarded as a painful ordeal, which earns those who endure it the felicity of the Blessed. In the twelfth century the abbot of Cluny, Peter the Venerable, thus describes the nuns of the priory of Marcigny as "secluded in the salutary cloister and so to speak buried in this vivifying sepulcher, but expecting in exchange of their imprisonment eternal liberation and in the stead of their tomb the blessed resurrection."[35] It is easy to understand the relevance of the parallel recently drawn by historians between *carcer* and *claustrum*, the prison and the monastery, the former being little used for punitive ends until the eighteenth century, while the latter experiences a rapid expansion from the end of the first millennium on. This parallel is all the more fascinating since, after having long cohabited, the two institutions began to overlap and even substitute one for another when, after the French Revolution, the state turned the abbeys and monasteries into public goods and used them to detain criminals. The decline of monastic institutions, which had started before 1789, thus narrowly preceded the advent of the correctional institution, which was the product of revolutionary imagination. Ironically, on the point of falling in abeyance, places of religious confinement thus had a second life, this time as places for carceral confinement. By the 1860s half the French long-stay correctional facilities were abbeys or convents of the ancient régime.

In this respect the birth of the prison has long been presented as both the sign and the result of a humanization of punishment. The ideals of the Enlightenment, Cesare Beccaria's penal reformism, John Howard's philanthropic activism, and Jeremy Bentham's architectural utopia seemed concretized in the carceral institution, where physical retribution was replaced by moral correction, executions by education, and cruelty by discipline. Nowhere was this politics pushed as far as in the Jacksonian penitentiaries—a word definitely telling of the Christian influence—from 1820 on. As observed by David Rothman, the impassioned debates that opposed the champions of the "congregate model" at Auburn penitentiary, in New York State, where inmates were alone at night but worked and ate together in complete silence during the day, and the advocates of the "separate model" of Pennsylvania, epitomized by the Eastern State penitentiary, where inmates were constantly isolated in their cell without any contact with others, should not overshadow the deep similarities existing between the two projects.[36] For both of them, the idea was to substitute the experience of reclusion for the burning of the whip, psychic suffering for physical pain, salutary labor for pernicious idleness, and beneficial solitude for dangerous promiscuousness. The desire to punish and the hope of reform were thus reconciled.

Sent by the French government to study this system, Gustave de Beaumont and Alexis de Tocqueville came back from their mission seduced by its innovation and wrote an appreciative report. Yet when he undertook a similar journey ten years later, Charles Dickens was appalled by moral torments which he described as worse than physical torture. In fact, as shown by Rebecca McLennan, who speaks of the development of a system of "penal servitude," a major difference between the two prisons resided in the exploitation of the abundant and captive workforce that was aggressively put in place at Auburn but never adopted in Philadelphia.[37] The success of the model of the state of New York made it prosper and spread all over the country, whereas its historic rival was never taken up by other correctional institutions. This conspicuous alliance of the Christian morality and the Enlightenment philanthropy of the conceivers with the pragmatic realism and the manufacturing capitalism of the operators continued until the end of the nineteenth century, when progressive currents succeeded in imposing a vision of the prison system more in conformity with the principles of modern democracy.

The genealogy I have outlined therefore offers a critical perspective on the least discussed and even less analyzed part of punishment, namely the infliction of pain, which, as we have seen, remains the core of its definition—the only element of the classical theory that resists the empirical test. The shift from an affective economy of the debt, in which the sentiments of vengeance were channeled through various forms of restitution and compensation, to a moral economy of punishment, in which committing an offense calls for a retribution supposed to redeem the offender, is the major fact to take into account when reflecting on the central place occupied by suffering in the act of punishing. This reading, it should be noted, is diametrically opposed to Durkheim's main thesis, according to which the evolution from the mechanical solidarity of traditional societies to the organic solidarity of modern societies was accompanied by a parallel move from a legal system relying on repression and suffering to a legal system relying on restitution and cooperation.[38] Ethnological studies, since Malinowski, and historical approaches, after Simmel, have shown that restitution was essential to Trobriand Islanders in the early twentieth century as well as Anglo-Saxons in the second half of the first millennium. Needless to add, the contemporary world is not exempt from repression as the prison population is in constant progression.

In fact the genealogical approach reveals a former response to the violation of norms and rules that has almost become foreign to us, as the association between punishment and suffering seems self-evident today. Certainly since medieval times many things have changed. The moral economy of punishment has undergone substantial transformations as a result of the secularization of the institutions that impose retributions and of the law on which they rely. Nevertheless the ideological structures persist. In contrast to the common opinion according to which "the current evolution of criminal law was designed against the Churches and their theology," Paul Ricœur asserts that "all present trends in criminal law, albeit apparently anti-religious, are perhaps a means to rediscover another meaning of penitence and punishment."[39] Among the examples he provides are the substitution of offense for sin and of amendment for expiation, in which he sees a felicitous improvement attesting to a return to real Christian values. Whether we agree or not with his normative stance and rejoice or not with him about the rediscovery of penitence, we must acknowledge the relevance of this reflection on the trace left by religion in contemporary criminal law but reconsider it from a critical perspective.

Indeed in the same way as, against the idea that Western modernity would be characterized by the separation of the religious and the political, Claude Lefort proposes an analysis of the "permanence of the theologico-political," I argue, against the conception of secularized legal institutions and criminal law, that there is a permanence of the theologico-juridical.[40] The illuminating questions raised by Lefort could in fact be reformulated by merely substituting *law* for *politics* and *penal system* for *political realm* in the following passage: "Can we say that religion has simply disappeared in the face of politics without asking ourselves what its investment in the political realm once meant? And do we not have to assume that it was so profoundly invested therein as to have become unrecognizable to those who believe its effects to have been exhausted?" The exploration of this "hidden part of social life," generally ignored or disavowed, could allow us to think of a penal theology in the same way as a political theology was conceived. The project would be to uncover the numerous translations of theological concepts into modern penology.

From this perspective, and with regard to the proposed genealogy of punishment, three elements would seem particularly pertinent: the individualization of the sentence, which prolongs the personalization of the guilt via the sin (versus the ancient collective logic of the debt); the infliction of suffering, which emerges from the exaltation of pain in both Christology and martyrology (versus the financial compensation of the damage); the discourse of moral reform, which revives the theology of redemption (versus the reparation within a broader circulation of goods and persons). These three elements offer a framework to recover lost religious traces in contemporary secularized laws and institutions. But they obviously do not account for the variations in time, at the whim of changes in policies and legislations, and the sometimes considerable contrasts in space, from one country, even one city, to the next. Contradictory trends do exist, indeed, with, for instance, the development of a so-called new penology, which claims somehow to demoralize and technicize penalty by considering populations rather than individuals and probability rather than culpability, by dismissing the relevance of suffering to privilege a managerial approach to institutions and their agents, finally by considering that the objective is not to amend the criminal but to reduce criminality—all elements that contradict point by point those previously mentioned.[41] Yet, however significant they may be, the swirls of these regularly announced changes should not eclipse the tidal wave of the enduring phenomena. The genealogy of punishment and the penal theology that it invites imagining are in that regard instruments to think critically about continuities as well as ruptures—and perhaps even potentialities for the future.

If, at the end of this long journey across ethnographic and genealogical terrains, we return for a last time to Hart's definition, we thus realize that punishment can sanction an offense or not, affect an offender or not, be administered by those other than the offender or not, and be imposed by an authority constituted by a legal system or not. That the criteria supposed to circumscribe the normative framework of punishment be so fragile, as their proponent himself had suggested, evidence how intellectually risky and politically problematic may be a definitive answer to the question: What is punishment? However, this conclusion should not discourage the researcher or the citizen. The tension between the normative and critical perspectives is, on the contrary, heuristic, from an analytical point of view, and constructive, from the perspective of action. It invites us to confront more rigorously what ought to be and what actually is, so as to better question both—instead of being content with merely asserting the former and describing the latter, as is too often the case.

Finally, of the five criteria constituting the initial definition, only one remains: the infliction of pain, which, as the genealogical inquiry reveals, has not always been part of the reaction to the violation of social codes and largely results from a Christian-inspired moralization of punishment. Such a conclusion therefore calls for a new interrogation: How does one justify this imposition of suffering in response to a wrong? In other words: Why does one punish?

Notes

1. H. L. A. Hart, "The Presidential Address: Prolegomenon to the Principles of Punishment," *Proceedings of the Aristotelian Society* 60 (1959–60): 1–26, esp. 4–5.

2. Kelly Hannah Moffat and Mona Lynch, "Theorizing Punishment's Boundaries: An Introduction," *Theoretical Criminology* 16.2 (2012): 19–21.

3. Thomas Aquinas, *The Summa Theologica*, trans. Fathers of the English Dominican Province (ia.eu/03d/1225-1274,_Thomas_Aquinas,_Summa_Theologiae_%5B1%5D,_EN.pdf; first published in 1265–74), part 2-2, question 108, article 1.

4. Robert Nozick, "Retributive Punishment," in *Philosophical Explanations* (Cambridge, MA: Harvard University Press, 1981), 363–97, esp. 366–68.

5. Leo Zaibert, "Punishment and Revenge," *Law and Philosophy* 25 (2006): 81–118, esp. 82–85.

6. Danielle Allen, *The World of Prometheus: The Politics of Punishing in Democratic Athens* (Princeton, NJ: Princeton University Press, 2000), 25–35.

7. Émile Durkheim, *The Division of Labor in Society*, trans. W. D. Hall (New York: Free Press, 1984; first published in French in 1893), 47.

8. Shannon Portillo and Danielle Rudes, "Construction of Justice at the Street Level," *Annual Review of Law and Society* 10 (2014): 321–34.

9. Anistia Internacional Brasil, *You Killed My Son: Homicides by Military Police in the City of Rio de Janeiro* (Rio de Janeiro: Amnesty International, 2015); Karen Lema, "Philippines Drug War Deaths Climb to 1,800: U.S. Deeply Concerned," Reuters, August 22, 2016, http://www.reuters.com/article/us-philippines-duterte-un-killings-idUSKCN10X0IS; "The Guardian View on Killings by US Police: Why We Must Keep Counting," *Guardian*, December 31, 2015; "Number of Executions since 1976," Death Penalty Information Center, last updated November 9, 2017, http://www.deathpenaltyinfo.org/executions-year; Jerome Karabel, "The Other Capital Punishment", *Huffpost Politics*, December 10, 2014.

10. New York Civil Liberties Union, "Stop-and-Frisk Data," n.d., http://www.nyclu.org/content/stop-and-frisk-data; Noah Berlastky, "When Chicago Tortured," *The Atlantic*, December 17, 2014; Spencer Hackerman, "Homan Square Revealed: How Chicago Police 'Disappeared' 7,000 People," *Guardian*, October 19, 2015.

11. Anthony Flew, "The Justification of Punishment," *Philosophy* 29.111 (1954): 291–307, esp. 291.

12. United Nations, High Commissioner for Human Rights, "Punitive Demolitions Destroy More than Homes in Occupied Palestinian Territory," December 28, 2015, http://www.ohchr.org/EN/NewsEvents/Pages/PunitivedemolitionsinOPT.aspx; Lizzie Dearden, "Tel Aviv Attack: Israeli Authorities Seal Off West Bank and Gaza as UN Condemns 'Collective Punishment' of Palestinians," *Independent*, June 10, 2016; Marijn Nieuwenhuis, "Skunk Water: Stench as a Weapon of War," *OpenDemocracy*, December 17, 2015, https://www.opendemocracy.net/marijn-nieuwenhuis/skunk-water-stench-as-weapon-of-war; Marjorie Cohn, "Israel Inflicts Illegal Collective Punishment on Gaza," *World Post*, n.d., http://www.huffingtonpost.com/marjorie-cohn/israel-palestine-collective-punishment_b_5589208.html.

13. Nicola Perugini and Neve Gordon, *The Human Right to Dominate* (Oxford: Oxford University Press, 2015).

14. Ram Subramanian, Ruth Delaney, Stephen Roberts, Nancy Fishman, and Peggy McGarry, *Incarceration's Front Door: The Misuse of Jails in America* (New York: Vera Institute for Justice, 2015), 4–30; *Statistique mensuelle des*

personnes écrouées et détenues en France au 1er juillet 2016 (Paris: Direction de l'administration pénitentiaire, 2016).

15. Julie Seman, "When Innocence Is No Defense," *New York Times*, August 12, 2015; Alec Karakatsanis, "President Obama's Department of Injustice," *New York Times*, August 18, 2015.

16. Alfred de Zayas, "Human Rights and the Indefinite Detention," *International Review of the Red Cross* 87.857 (2005): 15–38; Kate Martin and Joe Onek, *"Enemy Combatants," the Constitution and the Administration's "War on Terror"* (Washington, DC: American Constitution Society for Law and Policy, 2004).

17. Géraldine Duthé, Angélique Hazard, Annie Kensey, and Jean-Louis Pan Ké Shon, "L'augmentation du suicide en prison en France depuis 1945," *Bulletin Épidémiologique Hebdomadaire* 47–48 (2011): 504–8.

18. Les Johnston, "What Is Vigilantism?," *British Journal of Criminology* 36.2 (1996): 220–36; Sarah Jane Cooper-Knocks and Olly Owen, "Between Vigilantism and Bureaucracy: Improving Our Understanding of Police Work in Nigeria and South Africa," *Theoretical Criminology* 19.3 (2015): 355–75.

19. Émile Durkheim, *The Division of Labor in Society*, trans. W. D. Hall (New York: Free Press, 1984; first published in French in 1893), esp. 46.

20. Hart, "The Presidential Address," 6.

21. Friedrich Nietzsche, *On the Genealogy of Morals*, trans. Walter Kaufman (New York: Vintage Books, 1989; first published in German in 1887), esp. Second essay, sections 4 and 5.

22. William Shakespeare, *The Merchant of Venice* (New York: Simon & Schuster, New Folger Shakespeare Library, 2010), Act 3, Scene 1.

23. Émile Benveniste, *Indo-European Language and Society*, trans. Elizabeth Palmer (Miami: University of Miami Press, 1973; first published in French in 1969), esp. Book 1-5, Book 4-5, and Book 6-5.

24. Félix Gaffiot, *Dictionnaire Latin Français* (Paris: Hachette, 1934), 1193–94.

25. Alain Rey, *Dictionnaire historique de la langue française* (Paris: Robert, 2006), 3:3226.

26. Kalervo Oberg, "Crime and Punishment in Tlingit Society," *American Anthropologist* 36.2 (1934): 145–56, esp. 146–47.

27. Leopold Pospisil, "Modern and Traditional Administration of Justice in New Guinea," *Journal of Legal Pluralism* 19 (1981): 93–116, esp. 96, 110.

28. Arzoo Osanloo, "When Blood Has Spilled: Gender, Honor, and Compensation in Iranian Criminal Sanctioning," *Political and Legal Anthropology Review* 35.2 (2012): 308–26.

29. Moses Finley, "La servitude pour dettes," *Revue Historique de Droit Français et Étranger*, 4th series, 43 (1965): 160–84.

30. Judy Gaughan, *Murder Was Not a Crime* (Austin: University of Texas, 2010), esp. 3.

31. Georg Simmel, *The Philosophy of Money*, trans. Tom Bottomore and David Frisby (London: Routledge & Kegan Paul, 1978; 1st German publication 1907), esp. 355–66.

32. Michel Foucault, *Théories et institutions pénales: Cours au Collège de France, 1971–1972* (Paris: Hautes Études, Gallimard-Seuil, 2015), esp. 114–19 and 132–39.

33. Valérie Toureille, *Crime et châtiment au Moyen Âge, V*^{e}*–XV*^{e} *siècle* (Paris: Seuil, 2013), esp. 247 and 305.

34. Pieter Spierenburg, "The Body and the State: Early Modern Europe," in *The Oxford History of the Prison: The Practice of Punishment in Western Society*, ed. Norval Morris and David Rothman (Oxford: Oxford University Press, 1995), 44–70, esp. 50.

35. Isabelle Heullant-Donat, Julie Claustre, and Élisabeth Lusset, *Enfermements: Le cloître et la prison V*^{e}*–XVIII*^{e} *siècle* (Paris: Publications de la Sorbonne, 2011), esp. 15–35, 153–67.

36. David Rothman, *The Discovery of Asylum: Social Order and Disorder in the New Republic* (1971; New Brunswick, NJ: Aldine Transaction, 2008), 79–109.

37. Rebecca McLennan, *The Crisis of Imprisonment: Protest, Politics, and the Making of the American Penal State, 1776–1941* (Cambridge, UK: Cambridge University Press, 2008), esp. 469–72.

38. Durkheim, *The Division of Labour in Society*, esp. 29.

39. Paul Ricœur, "Le droit de punir," *Cahiers de Villemétrie* 6 (1958): 2–21, esp. 2.

40. Claude Lefort, "Permanence of the Theologico-Political?," in *Democracy and Political Theory* (Cambridge, UK: Polity, 1991; first published in French in 1986), 148–87, esp. 150.

41. Malcolm Feeley and Jonathan Simon, "The New Penology: Notes on the Emerging Strategy of Corrections and Its Implications," *Criminology* 30.4 (1992): 449–74.

Chapter 2: Why Does One Punish?

Legal theorists deem important the inaugural distinction between the definition and the justification of punishment, the former being a prerequisite, which is supposed to be value-neutral, whereas the latter represents the more substantial element of the concept, which relies on value judgments. We must know what we are talking about before attempting to argue on a moral basis about its raison d'être, philosophers and jurists say, including Hart.[1] That the division of the intellectual task be so easy, however, and that it even be possible, we may doubt, and as we have seen, we can also wonder about the neutrality of the operation, which consists in deciding what is punishment.[2] The fact that most definitions imply a pain inflicted on the offender already supposes an implicit justification that this suffering is necessary. If this is the case, what is this justification?

As John Rawls observes, "The trouble has not been that people disagree as to whether or not punishment is justifiable. Most people have held that, freed from certain abuses, it is an acceptable institution. Only a few have rejected punishment entirely, which is rather surprising when one considers all that can be said against it. The difficulty is with the justification of punishment: various arguments for it have been given by moral philosophers, but so far none of them has won any sort of general acceptance."[3] A consensus thus seems to exist about the fact that punishment is justified, but things gets complicated when one has to explain why. In fact this very question, *Why?*, can be understood in two different ways: prescriptive (Why should one punish?) and descriptive (Why do people actually punish?). In the first case, what is expected is a theoretical justification provided a priori, generally by moral philosophers or legal scholars. In the second, what is anticipated is an empirical justification given a posteriori, which can be subjective, provided by the agent, or objective, proposed by the researcher. Although the limits between the prescriptive and the descriptive, between the subjective and the objective, are never perfectly drawn, I will present how the different normative approaches justify punishment and how the idiographic method relying on case studies disturbs, contradicts, and enriches these justifications.

Two theories of justification prevail in the philosophical and legal literature. For utilitarians, only the consequences that punishment can have from the point of view of society should be taken into account. For retributivists, only the act that has been committed should be taken into account, punishment being its just deserts. Focused on reducing criminality, the former are essentially looking toward the future. Concentrated on the expiation of the crime, the latter are mainly oriented toward the past. Utilitarianism tends to dominate in the intellectual realm and the public sphere when progressive opinions thrive. Retributivism tends to impose itself in periods when conservative and reactionary ideas prosper. During recent decades the second has tended to eclipse the first.

Utilitarianism, as a subtype of consequentialist ethics, holds that general principles and specific actions are assessed according to their predictable effects. The primary goal of these principles and actions is to increase the quantity of happiness in the world. Only what contributes to this goal is useful, and in terms of criminal law, punishment is justified only when it produces a more positive balance of good over evil than any alternative measure. For Jeremy Bentham, who first theorized this approach in 1780, "all punishment in itself is bad" since it causes suffering, and "it ought to be allowed only insofar as it promises to exclude some greater evil," on condition that there is not a less costly manner to obtain a similar result.[4] Consequently "punishment ought not to be inflicted" when it is "groundless," "ineffective," "unprofitable," or "needless." Its immediate end is to prevent criminal acts: those of the offender as well as of the entire community. This prevention can be realized in three ways: by intervening on the offender's "will" with the objective of "reforming him"; by controlling his "physical power" with the intention of "disabling him"; by making "an example" so as to "influence the conduct of others." There might be a "collateral goal" of punishment, "that of providing pleasure or satisfaction to the injured party where there is one," but this should never be a justification as such. Thus defined, the theory has varied little with time. In its contemporary version, the rationales at work are, under another designation, those described by Bentham: rehabilitation, incapacitation, and deterrence. While utilitarianism is sometimes contested on theoretical grounds because of the possibility of condemning an innocent for the great good of society, it is at the empirical level that the most interesting discussions have taken place. Indeed since consequences are supposed to be assessed, proving efficacy is decisive.

As far as it limits the offender's ability to act, incapacitation seems the most obvious candidate in that regard. It can operate in three ways: execution, removal, and incarceration. The death penalty has considerably declined worldwide in recent decades and is now in force in only forty-three of the almost two hundred countries of the United Nations; it remains legal in thirty-four of the fifty states of the United States. Deportation has frequently been used in the past for criminals, the most famous example being Australia, the colonization of which was undertaken by 160,000 convicts from Britain; following this example, France created its penal colonies in Guyana and New Caledonia, which remained active until the mid-twentieth century. Imprisonment is today the most common form of exclusion: globally over ten million people are incarcerated, almost one-fourth of them in the United States; the constant progression of the carceral population is principally due to punitive policies and practices that send more people behind bars for longer periods of time. Yet even under these conditions, the incapacitation lasts only the time of the stay. Is it effective, then? Based on available studies, that is doubtful. As an illustration, the decrease in thefts concomitant with the increase in prison sentences in California during the 1980s and 1990s could suggest a positive relationship between the two trends, but a closer analysis shows that the decline in offenses essentially concerned juveniles, for whom sentences had not been harsher, while among adults, who had been more severely sanctioned, criminal activities did not diminish.[5] Commonsense logic was deceptive.

For deterrence, which implies that the threat of punishment dissuades potential criminals, it is certainly an old idea, if we think of how public executions were staged and the convicts' bodies exposed in medieval societies and even later. Long neglected by criminologists precisely because it evoked this bygone age, it has attracted attention again when economists have integrated it in their rational actor model, according to which, before acting, criminals are supposed to weigh the benefits expected from their deed against the costs of the anticipated sanction and the risk of being arrested. However, the passage from this theoretical model to empirical reality is far from convincing. Actually dissuasion is assessed mostly in two ways. At the individual level, one measures recidivism rates in cohorts after the infliction of the punishment. In France, for example, a survey of seven thousand convicts sentenced to prison has established that repeat offenses were less frequent when sentences were adjusted either before the incarceration or toward the end of the stay in prison, even when the criminal record, the type of offense and the length of the sentence are taken into account; these conclusions suggest that avoiding imprisonment or shortening its duration reduces the risk of repeat offense. At the collective level, one evaluates crime rates in the general population as changes are introduced in penal policies or practices. In the United States, for instance, the spectacular decline in homicides and thefts in the 1990s has been discussed in relation to the increase in police presence on the streets or to the doubling of the prison population. But the comparison with Canada, where a similar trend in crime has been observed during that same period, while the number of officers and the carceral demographics were both decreasing by one-tenth, seems to invalidate the hypothesis of a beneficial impact of policing and incarceration.[6] For the most part, the results of these studies, sometimes passionately debated, refute the economic model of utility maximization, since less constraining measures and less repressive policies appear to have better results than opposite options.

Finally, rehabilitation, after having served as the main justification for incarceration at various moments in the history of prisons, notably at the beginning of the nineteenth century in Jacksonian penitentiaries and in the middle of the twentieth century with the penal welfarism movement, has gone through a long period of discredit since the 1970s. The idea that punishment can transform and meliorate the criminal, make him conscious of the seriousness of his act, and, thanks to educational and social resources, facilitate his reentry was then delegitimized as it was deemed ineffective under the "nothing works" motto of conservative intellectuals and politicians, especially in Britain and the United States. Recently, however, rehabilitation has found new advocates and statistical studies have established its benefits in terms of recidivism when compared to classical punitive methods.[7] The announcement of its death thus appears to have been premature.

The three rationales of the utilitarian justification refer to distinct approaches: physical for incapacitation, psychological for deterrence, moral but also educational and social for rehabilitation. Whereas they seem clearly differentiated from an analytical point of view, they partially overlap, in particular when the assessment of their efficacy is conducted. Should a decline in crime associated with an expansion of prison population, to the extent that one admits the existence of a link between the two phenomena, be attributed to the removal of criminals from society, to individuals renouncing crime for fear of sanctions, or to criminals reforming as a result of reentry programs? Studies provide no definitive answer. But retributivists do not have this sort of doubt or even question. For them, punishment can be justified only by the crime committed.

Retributivism, as part of the deontological ethics, relies on the idea of obligation. It seems in principle much easier to defend since it supposes no external assessment of its social efficacy but simply the internal evaluation of its moral coherence. Indeed it asserts that, for justice to be done, those who have committed wrongdoings deserve to suffer. Punishment must be justified on this sole ground. The classical argument is developed by Kant: "Juridical punishment can never be administered merely as means for promoting another good, either with regard to the criminal himself or to civil society, but must in all cases be imposed only because the individual on whom it is inflicted has committed a crime."[8] This principle derives from the categorical imperative that humans should never be treated solely as means but always also as ends in themselves. One cannot punish for the greater good of society, but only because the person has been "found guilty and punishable," since "if justice and righteousness perish, human life would no longer have any value in the world." As for the way to implement this principle equality must guide "the mode and measure of punishment." Consequently "the right of retaliation" implies that "whoever has committed murder must die." Such right is based on the idea that "the undeserved evil which one commits on another is to be regarded as perpetrated against himself." In other words, the justice system tells the offender, "If you slander another, you slander yourself; if you steal from another, you steal from yourself; if you strike another, you strike yourself; if you kill another, you kill yourself." This radical version of retributivism dates back to the *lex talionis* of Babylonian and Hebrew laws, and, as we have seen, early Roman law developed instead a principle of reparation for the loss, while Islamic law combined both rationales.

Other versions of retributivism have been proposed, with different justifications for the penalty: restitution of the benefits unduly acquired by the offender, compensation of the damages done to the victim, satisfaction of the punitive affects generated by the wrongdoing among the population.[9] Two variants, which share some common grounds, deserve special attention. The first thesis asserts that the main function of punishment is expressive. According to Joel Feinberg, "punishment is a conventional device for the expression of attitudes of resentment and indignation, and of judgments of disapproval and reprobation, either on the part of the punishing authority himself or of those 'in whose name' the punishment is inflicted."[10] Its meaning is therefore essentially symbolic. Suffering as such does not suffice to characterize punishment. A form of reproach must be associated with it. As a consequence, the justification cannot reside in the mere equivalence between crime and sentence. It must rely on the equivalence between the crime and the condemnation that society wants to manifest, the latter depending on two elements regarding the former: "the amount of harm it generally causes and the degree to which people are disposed to commit it." Ultimately "pain should match guilt only insofar as its infliction is the symbolic vehicle of public condemnation." The second thesis somewhat extends the expressive function of punishment by focusing on its ethical implications. As Jean Hampton suggests, "We must link the point of the retributive response to the wrongfulness of the action."[11] Punishment can be justified not on the ground of the damage done to the victim but on the fact that the offender has committed a reprehensible action. Harm and wrong must be separated, as someone may be harmed without any wrong being committed, by a business competitor, for instance, and a wrong may be committed without anyone being harmed, in case of a failed attempt at murder, for example. The point of retribution is therefore not "correcting harms," which can be dealt with through reparation, but "righting wrongs," the wrongfulness of an action being that it is "an affront to the victim's value or dignity." Such "moral injuries" are attacks on "human worth" in general and on "the person's value" in particular, often based on inegalitarian prejudices. Only those deserve punishment.

These theses have the merit of integrating the symbolic, moral, and affective dimension of punishment. However, they describe an ideal world, which can be challenged with a reality principle. Indeed the public condemnation of a crime and the decision to punish it on this ground are not only related to its properties, notably the harm it has caused and the wrong it entails, but depends on power relations and tensions between meanings that change over time. Thus minor acts by "minor actors" can be more harshly sanctioned than major acts by "major actors," including when the latter victimize people and the former has no victim. Similarly a practice previously considered acceptable may be made an offense; an offense until then ignored may become an object of sanctions; and a sanction consisting of a fine may turn into a prison sentence, without the concerned acts having been modified.

But as is often the case in analytic philosophy, debates between utilitarians and retributivists have rather taken a fictional turn with fables proposing extreme cases or singular dilemmas either to prove their respective points or, more often, to refute that of their fancied opponent.[12] Thus H. J. McCloskey contests the utilitarian theory by imagining a sheriff who, after a crime has been committed, randomly arrests a black man "in order to stop a series of lynchings which he knew would occur if the guilty person were not immediately found, or believed to have been found," and, a little later, a man who, visiting an area where "a Negro rapes a white woman, and race riots occur as a result of the crime," concludes "that he has a duty to bear false testimony" by randomly accusing a black man so as to stop the collective violence. In these cases, which seem to reveal a conspicuous racial tropism of the author, the utilitarian is supposed to cause the punishment of an innocent individual for a greater collective good. Symmetrically, to contradict the retributivist theory, Gertrude Ezorsky imagines "a world in which punishing has no further effects worth achieving," so that "the criminal, punished, is perfectly ready to go out and commit his crime all over again," while "ordinary men are not deterred in the slightest from crime by the threat of punishment" and "victims of crime have no desire for retaliation, and the pleasure of vengeance is unknown." Moreover if a "painless but expensive pill" able to cure "propensity to crime" is discovered, the utilitarians will adopt it, while the retributivists will prefer to keep on punishing so as to stick to their principles, with the result that, as juries are not infallible, they will end up killing innocents. This improbable parable is meant to return the compliment regarding the most common criticism against utilitarianism. Of course both utilitarians and retributivists have good arguments to disprove the supposed flaws uncovered by their respective opponents.

It is not certain, however, that these intellectual jousts do justice to the complex and serious issues related to the justification of punishment. By restricting the reflection to the confrontation between the two theses and even to debates within each strand, as is habitually the case, the risk is that one will overlook two elements. First, although they seem conceptually incompatible, these justifications can in fact be combined, either theoretically or empirically. On one side, several authors have noted the overlap between utilitarianism and retributivism, and some have even formulated hybrid versions, generally designated as pluralist. On the other side, in the public sphere, those who discuss this question, in particular politicians, do not attach great importance to the subtleties of philosophical reasoning; for instance, the advocates of penal populism use both arguments of deterrent effects and just deserts to defend their position. Second, beyond their divergences the two theories and their variants have two traits in common, which logically ensue from their normative stance. On the one hand, they do not content themselves with the analysis of justification; they contribute to the justification. On the other hand, they do not depict real situations, including when they rely on examples in the form of allegories and apologues, and do not account for the justifications that agents actually give to themselves and to others for their decision to punish.

The most lucid reflection in that regard comes again from Nietzsche: "Today it is impossible to say for certain why people are really punished."[13] Not because the ultimate cause would be hidden, but on the contrary because too many reasons may be found in the multiple situations in which one resorts to punishment. It can be a "means of rendering harmless, of preventing further harm," a "means of inspiring fear of those who determine and execute the punishment," a "recompense to the injured party for the harm done," the "isolation of a disturbance of equilibrium, so as to guard against any further spread," a "repayment for the advantages the criminal has enjoyed hitherto," the "expulsion of a degenerate element," a "festival, namely as the rape and mockery of a finally defeated enemy," the "marking of memory whether for him who suffers the punishment or for those who witness its execution," the "payment of a fee stipulated by the power that protects the wrongdoer from the excesses of revenge," a "compromise with revenge in its natural state," or a "declaration of war and a war measure against an enemy of peace," among other reasons. This disparate catalog evidently contrasts with the logical dualism of the alternative between utilitarianism and retributivism. However, it is telling less of a contradiction with classical philosophical and legal theories than of a difference in "perspective," to use a Nietzschean concept. Indeed with the *Genealogy of Morals*, we are not any more in the pure realm of ideas and the law but in the impure region of the obscure motives of crime and punishment—the world of Dostoevsky more than the universe of Bentham and Kant, so to speak.

A similar shift is operated when one leaves the theoretical domain to enter empirical situations. As evidence I will take three brief ethnographic cases illustrating forms of punishment in the street, in court, and in prison.

First scene. Three adolescents are talking and laughing joyously in a small square near the hostel of the youth protection service, where they stay. Like the other minors residing in the three-floor house, they have been placed in this institution by a juvenile judge either because they have committed a misdemeanor or because they are deemed endangered. The three teenagers are of African origin. Two police officers on patrol stop by and ask for their papers. Such a check is banal but illegal, since there is no indication of a crime being or having been committed and since it is moreover established that such a stop is often based on racial profiling. The adolescents present their travel passes, which should be regarded as sufficient since they contain their name and photograph. Not satisfied, the police demand their identification cards. The adolescents, who do not have these documents with them, explain that they live in the hostel some twenty yards away and propose the officers accompany them to fetch them. The police ruthlessly refuse and threaten to take the boys to the precinct for further verification. This is an obvious abuse of authority since the travel pass should have sufficed and the visit to the hostel would have been an alternative if they had doubts. Panicked at the prospect of being taken in, one of the teenagers escapes, runs to his lodging, takes the requested card, and swiftly returns to prove his good faith. But the reception is not what he expects. The police scold him harshly, using racist slurs while slapping him. Alerted by the shouting, one of the social workers of the service goes outside, only to hear one of the officers threaten the boy by saying "I'm going to kneecap you!" and yell at him "You're a failure in your family! You're a failure at school! You little faggot!" Not without difficulty, the social worker interposes herself and finally brings the adolescent back to the hostel. There, with the director of the institution, she tries to convince him to file a complaint against the officer, telling him it is important to defend his rights. Still shaken and distressed by the humiliating and aggressive handling he just endured, the teenager keeps repeating in a low voice that it does not matter. Obviously he knows how much weight the word of a black minor under the care of a youth protection service would carry compared to the word of the police, how easily his complaint could be reversed into a case against him for resisting arrest, and in the end how costly it could be to try to assert his rights. Interrupting the discussion, he impatiently returns to his room.

Second scene. A thin man in his mid-thirties, looking lost in the impressively vast space of the regional courthouse, stands in the defendant's box. Haggard after twenty-four hours spent in custody, he faces charges for driving without a license and insurance. As he was on his way home, he had a minor car accident: he crashed into a signpost and drove off, not realizing that his license plate had fallen off. The police did not have difficulty identifying the vehicle, which officially belonged to the man's wife, and summoned him, but he did not go to the precinct. Four months later two officers came to his apartment to arrest him as he was leaving for work. At the trial the judge notes with irritation that it is not the first time he has had dealings with the justice system. Indeed he has already received nineteen citations in the past fifteen years, mostly for similar offenses. He has been sentenced to prison four times, generally for between two and four months. Born one of seven children in a Roma family, he dropped out of school, had a series of temporary jobs, and finally stabilized his professional situation for some time as a delivery driver. Under the usual pressure of this sort of activity, and with the multiplication of speed cameras, he was caught several times for excessive speed, received points, and lost his license. He nevertheless continued working and was arrested on several occasions while driving. The first time he was incarcerated, he lost his job. From then on, his life became precarious again. After his last stay in prison, he remained unemployed for several months but was eventually hired in a warehouse. When he was arrested after the car accident, he was on the verge of signing a long-term contract with his company. The trial lasts only thirty-five minutes and concludes with a verdict of six months in prison and payment of damages. The defendant is handcuffed and taken to the local jail. In my conversation with her afterward, the judge, disheartened, comments, "We don't know what to do in these cases. We're helpless. We know he'll do it again, but we still have to apply the punishment. With his previous convictions, what else could we do?" When I meet the man in prison three days later, he is bitter: "Sure, driving without a license is illegal, but you can't call it a serious crime. It's not right that you end up together with burglars and rapists just for that. I've been inside four times and I have been offered a lot of stuff. I've even been straight up to join robberies. There are Islamists here too; they try to recruit us." He is persuaded that if the sentence has been so severe it is because he is a Roma. After a brief pause, he adds, "I'm really pissed, because I was putting my life back together again. I had a job. I had my kids." His wife is on the verge of giving birth to their fourth child. His eldest son is having behavioral problems in school. Six months later I have the surprise of bumping into him in jail; by then he should have been out due to automatic sentence reductions. A guard later tells me that he had actually been released after serving his time, but that only three weeks later he was arrested again and sentenced to ten months in prison for domestic violence.

Third scene. An inmate is brought into the cramped room adjacent to the solitary confinement unit, where disciplinary board hearings take place. Behind a small wooden podium, the sinister-looking man faces the three persons who will judge him: a deputy warden, a correctional officer, and a civil society volunteer. He is accused of making racial slurs against a black guard as he was returning from the yard several weeks earlier. Normally, in such a situation, the complaint of the officer is detailed and the report of an investigation conducted by a superior is appended. In this particular case, the only evidence is the statement of the correctional officer, whose name is not even revealed to the prisoner. There are no witnesses, no specifics, no inquiry. Knowing neither his accuser's identity nor the circumstances of the alleged offense, the inmate seems disconcerted. "Don't even know who the guy is," he mutters.

Perhaps by excess of confidence, he has not requested a lawyer and keeps repeating that he does not remember anything of the episode, about which the disciplinary board is incapable of providing any information. For lack of substantial elements in the file, the deputy warden contents himself with enumerating the thirty-some episodes of misconduct since the defendant's incarceration, as if they could serve as evidence for the supposed recent altercation. To his dismay, the prisoner is sent back to a cell nearby without having even been asked to defend himself. During the deliberation, a trainee correction lieutenant comments to me that, in the facility where he has been working as a guard for ten years, they would never have made a decision on such a vague accusation. Yet when the prisoner is brought back into the room, he is told that he is sentenced to seven days of solitary confinement. In an irrepressible act of rage, he punches and breaks the podium behind which he stands. Three guards who were waiting outside rush into the room, pin him against the wall, and handcuff him. While he loudly protests the unfairness of the decision, they take him to his punitive cell. The civil society volunteer who sits on the board tells me in an aside that if the man were to appeal, he would definitely win his case. But the inmate is certainly not even aware of this possibility. Not only will he spend the next seven days in solitary confinement, but the incident will affect the granting of a sentence reduction, block the possibility of a temporary release, and delay his prospect of being released on parole. Multiple punishments for the same act are the rule in prison. Another deputy warden with whom I later speak makes it clear that, even when prison officials do not believe in the veracity of the guards' version, especially when the accusers are known for their aggressive behavior, they cannot afford to appear to disown the guards. "He who says that we decide on the sole basis of facts and the inmate's profile does not tell the truth." Commenting on sentences to solitary confinement delivered for minor offenses in a context of recent tensions in the prison, she adds that punishing prisoners, even when it is obvious that they have been harried and responded to provocations by an officer, serves to satisfy and appease the personnel. "It avoids the guards taking revenge on the prisoners," she straightforwardly explains.

These three cases illustrate the diversity and intricacy of the reasons that police officers, criminal judges, and prison wardens punish. Of course these examples do not exhaust all forms of punishment in law enforcement, judicial, and correctional institutions. In particular, one of the most common reasons worldwide for penalizing people is fiscal: either officially, through fines, or unofficially, through bribery, the police and more generally the penal system collect money, especially from the most vulnerable segments of society. Federal investigations conducted in the United States have shown the banality of well-structured networks among police officers, judges, jails, and municipalities, enabling the extortion of penalties and exertion of pressure on the poor belonging to ethnoracial minorities for insignificant or even fabricated offenses in order to increase the budget of the corresponding institutions.[14] As for the three reported situations in the street, in court, and in prison, I want to show the difficulty of simply answering the initial question: Why do people punish? when one is interpreting not imaginary dilemmas but actual cases.

In the first scene, the two law enforcement agents express their diffuse resentment against the three adolescents who embody the black youth of the housing projects—"the bastards," as the officers habitually call them, with the connotation of illegitimate birth associated with the word. But the combination of hostility and racism, which is common among the police working in low-income neighborhoods, has a moral resonance in this case: being under the supervision of the judicial institution, the teenagers have already had dealings with the penal system, either as delinquents or as victims or, more often than not, as both. Although the agents pretend to ignore that the boys live in the hostel, they evidently know where they come from, imagine what may have been their story, and mistreat them accordingly; hence the hassle about the documents, the threat to arrest them, the hurtful words, the slaps. For the officers, it is legitimate to punish the adolescents because of what they think of them. The psychological harassment and physical abuse not only allow the police to exert their discretionary power but also serve to inculcate a social order, as the youths are learning, through the repetition of similar experiences, their social position of racial and moral inferiority.

In the second scene, the judge wearily indicates that she was embarrassed by the case but felt that she had to issue a prison sentence for lack of alternative. In fact she was not constrained in her decision by the law since mandatory sentencing did not apply to this particular situation, and she does not even seem convinced of the efficacy of the verdict to prevent future offenses from being committed. Besides, she undoubtedly realizes that the incarceration will make the man lose his job, take him away from his family obligations, and render the living conditions of his wife and children more precarious. More than anything else the prison sentence seems to be the result of a judicial routine acquired in the course of hearings during which similar cases accumulate and alternative sanctions are rarely envisaged. As one of her colleagues later told me, when law-makers imposed mandatory minimum prison time for repeat offenders in 2007 under a right-wing government, judges initially protested in the name of the individualization of sentences and the autonomy of their decisions, but they progressively got used to the new norm. Facts proved her right; five years later, when a newly appointed progressive minister of justice published a memorandum asking prosecutors to interpret the legislation with discernment, mentioning traffic violations as an example, of which the Roma inmate was a typical case, they did not abandon the inflexible practices they seemed to have adopted reluctantly shortly before, and the prison population continued to increase steadily.

In the third scene, the die seems cast from the start. The deputy warden who chairs the hearing knows that, despite the absence of evidence presented to the disciplinary board, the fact that it is an accusation of verbal abuse against a guard renders a sanction necessary. He anticipates that officers and inmates will scrutinize the judgment. An adjournment of the case for lack of established proof and investigation report or, worse, a clement verdict would be regarded on both sides as an implicit condemnation of the personnel. The prisoners would consider it a victory, and the news would soon be disseminated throughout the entire facility. The guards would interpret it as an absence of support from their institution, and their unions would probably express their anger. Under these conditions sentencing to solitary confinement is a tactic of peacekeeping in which showing fairness is secondary to maintaining order. No one is fooled: the wardens are realistic about its actual meaning; the prisoners view it as one more injustice of the system; even the guards seem aware of it, as they tell me in private that it was no surprise to them that this colleague would have been insulted or assaulted, considering the bully he was, but such acknowledgment would not have prevented them from protesting had the provoked inmate not been punished.

Do the theories of justification apply to these cases? Concerning the officers, it seems difficult to speak of retributivism, even if the punishment is harsh, since there is no offense committed, or of utilitarianism, as the only predictable consequence of the harassment is the adolescents' frustration and rancor. Regarding the judge, the brevity of the sentence and the de-socialization caused by the imprisonment do not advocate for the prisoner's incapacitation, dissuasion, or rehabilitation, which the repeat offense three weeks after his release appears to refute ex post; moreover, the disillusionment the magistrate expresses about her decision suggests that she even doubts the properly punitive rationale of the sanction for an act which, after all, has involved no victim other than the suspect himself. Finally, from the perspective of the disciplinary board, the penalty is less motivated by the alleged offense, since there is neither evidence nor even inner conviction of the jury, than by the previous incidents, although they have already been adjudicated and sanctioned; if one were tempted to be consequentialist by considering that the warden actually wants to preserve the peace in his institution, such analysis would amount to admitting the punishment of a possible innocent at the risk of generating other tensions.

Rather than attempting to impose a rigid theoretical framework on a complex empirical matter, we can use the three narratives to propose a distinct way of answering the question: Why punish? by dissociating the justifications, as they are provided by the agents (How do they justify their act of punishing?), and the interpretations, as they can be produced through a distanced analysis (How can one interpret these acts?). In the first case, the work of subjectivation of the agents aims at rendering acceptable, above all in their eyes, a problematic action. In the second case, the endeavor of objectivation of the analysis aims at rendering explicable, from a more general perspective, a type of equivocal action. These two operations are rarely distinguished. Yet the comprehension of scenes such as the three under discussion implies taking both of them into account.

The claim often heard from the police, that when they intervene in disadvantaged neighborhoods they merely enforce the law, must thus be placed in perspective with their assigned function, which consists in using their discretionary power to call to social order the purportedly dangerous classes. The firm conviction manifested by the magistrates, that they decide in complete independence and with reasonable fairness, must likewise be considered in light of an expanding culture of severity in criminal courts under the pressure of successive governments and public opinion, whose expectation is less about justice than about a socially differentiated distribution of penalties. The efforts of the corrections administration to provide disciplinary boards an appearance of respect of the rule of law must finally be analyzed in relation to the priority systematically given to the subordination of inmates and the security of the facilities. Justifications and interpretations therefore resonate with each other, and the local scenes must be understood as the products of broader social processes. The forms of punishment dispensed by the various agents are always inserted in the historical, cultural, and political context that makes them possible. Connecting the two levels—micro and macro, so to speak—is crucial to avoid focusing the explanation on individual conduct or decisions as well as to account for differences across space and time.

Until now both justifications and explanations of punishment have been presented in a rational frame—through the alternative between utilitarianism and retributivism in the normative theories, or through the diverse mechanisms of social order, bureaucratic routine, and institutional peacekeeping in the empirical descriptions. But the analysis must go further. Rationality does not exhaust the reasons people punish as they do. "Punishment constitutes an emotional reaction," affirms Durkheim. Trying to understand why it is always in excess, why shame doubles suffering, why disgrace supplements exclusion, why cruelty surfaces in the infliction of pain, he suggests that these unnecessary sanctions "are a form of additional tribulation that serves no purpose, or one whose sole reason is the need to repay evil with evil."[15] His reflection seems, however, to stop halfway, since it remains close to the radical retributivist theses, which rationalize vengeance as a response to an injury endured by an equivalent injury on the offender. It does suggest the pleasure in the infliction of pain, but does not name it.

It is once more in Nietzsche's writings that one can find the most exacting and lucid exploration of the emotional involvement in punishment: "the voluptuous pleasure '*de faire le mal pour le plaisir de le faire,*' the enjoyment of violation," he writes.[16] To punish is not merely to return evil for evil; it is to produce a gratuitous suffering, which adds to the sanction, for the mere satisfaction of knowing that the culprit suffers. In the act of punishing, something therefore resists rational analysis or, better said, resists being analyzed as rational: a drive, more or less repressed, to make suffer, which society tends to delegate to certain institutions and professions. Correctional institutions and officers occupy an extreme position in this process because they deal with a captive population that is already morally condemned, and they do so out of the sight of society. Let us consider the following tragic case.

On June 23, 2012, in a Miami prison, Darren Rainey, a fifty-year-old inmate suffering from schizophrenia and sentenced for cocaine possession, was punished for having defecated in his cell and refusing to clean it.[17] The sanction, called "the shower treatment" by the guards of the mental health unit, was commonly used with recalcitrant prisoners. The man was locked under a scalding-hot shower and, although he was screaming for help, was left shut up for more than an hour—until he died. According to witnesses, when his body was carried away, it was so burned that his skin had shriveled. Initially the police classified the death and the correctional institution took no sanction. It was only after a local newspaper publicized the case, revealing, on the basis of various testimonies from former personnel, that guards "taunted, tormented, abused, beat and tortured chronically mentally ill inmates on a regular basis" in order to provoke a response justifying punishment, that an inquiry was finally conducted. This was not the first time similar incidents ending in the death of an inmate after he had been mistreated were reported in this prison. In one case, three senior corrections department investigators were even sent to inquire; they described major dysfunctions with a systemic situation of abuse and corruption. But their report was dismissed by the state department of corrections, and they themselves were sidelined by their superiors. Only two years after Rainey's death were some minimal institutional changes undertaken, as the warden of the facility was discharged and two of the officers on duty on the day of the incident resigned, but no criminal charge was filed by the justice system. One more year was necessary for the medical examiner to present his report, which pronounced that the death had been accidental: the prisoner had died when he slipped and fell on the floor of the shower.

This tragedy is not isolated. Various reports stress the banality of physical, psychological, and sexual violence in the carceral world in the United States.[18] Even when an inmate dies, administrative sanctions are rare and criminal charges exceptional. Moreover the refusal given to lawyers, activists, and researchers who request permission to penetrate the prison world shows that the institution wants to avoid any sort of external presence and independent inquiry. This opaque and impenetrable universe can thus perpetuate neglect, abuse, brutality, and even torture with complete impunity. In fact it is often the institution itself that promotes cruelty and expects its personnel to be its executants. Solitary confinement, which was once imagined to be a possible path toward moral reform, has in the past decades revealed its bare truth: it is the mere imposition of a form of "social death," in Lisa Guenther's words, for months or years, such as in the case of a former Black Panther activist who spent forty-two years in solitary confinement. It is estimated that on any given day, more than eighty thousand prisoners are in restricted housing, with an average duration of five years for the twenty-five thousand individuals confined in supermax facilities. But the isolation and the radical de-socialization of the inmate is still not enough for the prison administration, which invents other torments, like the prohibition against lying down, leaning against the wall, or practicing physical exercise, as was the case for Chelsea Manning seventeen hours a day during her time in solitary confinement.[19] Consequently, since the corrections administration and the justice system not only tolerate these practices but also deny the right to assess them, when they do not simply encourage them, we can consider that they are actually part and parcel of the punishment: when judges sentence someone to prison, their decision entails much more than a deprivation of liberty, and they cannot not know it. But since the majority of politicians and citizens turn a blind eye to this reality, and even demand more severity in the law, more inflexibility from the magistrates, and harsher conditions for prisoners, we can argue that society does not content itself in authorizing these exactions; it perpetrates them by proxy. As Everett Hughes writes about the "unconscious mandate given by the rest of us" to the prison guard in the United States, "If, as sometimes happens, he is a man disposed to cruelty, there may be some justice in his feeling that he is only doing what others would like to do, if they but dared; and what they would do if they were in his place."[20] The indifference of the public, the silence of the political world, and the unwillingness of the penal system to change thus indicate that there exists a sort of license to exert, in its nakedness, an almost unbounded power to punish, namely as an indefinite right to inflict suffering.

Whereas it is certain that the United States represents an extreme case, it is far from being unique as fragmentary testimonies collected by human rights organizations and sometimes journalists across the world demonstrate. Yet it is difficult to imagine that such levels of cruelty would be possible or at least ignored or tolerated in European correctional institutions. The "Continental dignity and mildness" of the prison system in Europe, which James Q. Whitman contrasts with "American harshness," should certainly be relativized, but the differences he rightly emphasizes suggest that major variations exist within Western societies in terms of legal norms, institutional control, and, ultimately, respect of the rule of law regarding punishment. In fact, even within Europe, Nicola Lacey notes substantial differences, deeming "Britain's criminal justice system far less sensitive than that of Germany to the need to ensure humanity in punishment."[21] To consider that there is a limit clearly drawn between punitive policies and practices among nations would nevertheless be an error: the United States is certainly a borderline case, but it enlightens more broadly the emotional dimension of the drive to punish and the excesses it may generate. In the context of Europe, this component is repressed and the excesses are contained—which has not always been the case—but they remain present and could certainly revive. In this sense the penal and correctional system of the United States should be viewed as both exceptional and exemplary.

The pleasure associated with the act of punishing is not limited, however, to the tacit delegation of cruel acts to certain institutions and professions. It can also be felt personally by those who attend or even participate in the punishment. Lynching in the southern states under Jim Crow, stoning in certain Muslim countries applying sharia law, beating to death of presumed thieves by self-defense groups in sub-Saharan Africa and Latin America directly implicate the crowds that associate with them. But most of the time this troubling relationship takes indirect and attenuated forms. This is how one can interpret the success of numerous documentaries and reality shows, in which individuals are humiliated and mortified by police officers, judges, guards, journalists, even spectators for infractions they are suspected of having committed. One of these series sets up stings for "men caught soliciting sex from underage" girls and makes them confess on a hidden camera before being arrested by the police as they leave the "predator house." Another one films the daily life of maximum security prisons, focusing on their most violent scenes and most sinister prisoners, and even developing a new technology, a virtual reality headset, "which puts viewers inside America's jails and takes one of TV's most immersive series to a breathtaking new level."[22] Contrary to what one would have thought and, in a way, to what Foucault argued in his discussion of the death of the regicide Damiens, the spectacle of the punishment and its cruelty, which gathered people around the scaffolds where tortures and executions took place, has not disappeared; it has moved to the screen, including that of computers, as in the case of Allen Lee Davis's dramatic death by electrocution.[23] Surely this spectacle has been adapted to the demands of contemporary sensibilities: it has been softened; it does not have for its object the body, but the dignity of the person; it does not show a physical agony, but a social death. Yet it is a contemporary form of pornography, which arouses an ambiguous excitement at the sight of people suffering for their misdeeds. This is typically the case with the practice of public shaming by some magistrates in the United States, which consists in having the individual convicted of a misdemeanor carry a poster on which his offense is inscribed, in the same way as Hester Prynne, Nathaniel Hawthorne's adulterous heroine, had to wear on her chest the scarlet letter "A" for her crime.[24] But it is also what led the Islamic State to stage and publicize the beheading of its victims, thus anticipating, not without reason, the horror mixed with fascination that these images would not fail to elicit in Western countries. The cruel expressions of punishment and the pornographic manifestations of its spectacle are not aberrations. Their excesses—impulsive or deliberate—reveal that, in the act of punishing, there is always something that transcends pure rationality.

The three scenes previously recounted can indeed be reinterpreted in light of the emotions at play. For the police, the pleasure of intimidating, humiliating, abusing verbally and physically the adolescents is patent, as it is in numerous cases I observed during my fieldwork, when social inequality and ethnoracial distance added to power relationships. Thus, in other episodes, the officers overtly expressed their contentment at having disrupted a friendly party in a park by unjustified stop-and-frisks, and evidently enjoyed provoking a man in custody, desperate at the prospect of his imprisonment for an old sentence. In court, the affects may be less present in the decision, which does not satisfy the judge, than in the interactions that precede it, the admonition of the accused, the embarrassing comments on his social condition, and the offensive remarks on his opioid-replacement therapy redoubled by the lecture of the prosecutor and even the reproof of his attorney, all elements that go much further than the act of sanctioning an offender and reveal a delectation in the relationship of subjection thus generated. In the conversations I had with inmates whose trials I had attended, several told me how mortified they felt for having been treated in this way and how eager they were to see the end of this ordeal, with the anticipation of their incarceration being almost a relief. Finally, the trouble that is perceptible among the three persons on the disciplinary board in charge of adjudicating the case with an empty file shows their embarrassment, but the expectation of retribution expressed by the guards, even though guilt is not established, signals more unsettling sentiments. In fact during certain hearings, the president of the commission could also articulate statements the only objective of which seemed to be the belittlement of the prisoner or the emphasis on further negative consequences of the verdict. The excesses of the act of punishing therefore vary depending on the institutions, the contexts, the situations, and the persons; they can be manifest or hidden, explicit or ambiguous. But even in the supposedly most civilized forms of dispensing justice, a dark side remains.

Paraphrasing Georges Bataille, one could speak of the "accursed share" of punishment, thus transposing his idea of excess from the material to the emotional economy.[25] Of this accursed share, often disavowed, neither justifications nor interpretations can provide a full account.

The initial question: Why does one punish? has thus progressively been complicated. It first divided into two interrogations, one normative (Why should one punish?), the other analytical (Why do people actually punish?), the latter serving as an empirical test for the former. It then shifted toward another one: How do we punish?, which appeared to be indispensable to integrate the affective dimension of punishment eluded in usual rational approaches. Thus, from justification as pure reasoning, as it is discussed by philosophers and jurists, the reflection went to the justification by the agents (How do they account for what they do when they punish?) and the interpretation by the observer (How can one account for the various contexts and meanings of the act of punishing?), ending with the exploration of the obscure or, better said, obscured part (How much is the pleasure of making or seeing suffer an element of the act of punishing?), the one most profoundly buried and most difficult to even name.

Having arrived at this final stage, we could now reverse the direction of the reading and consider the philosophical and legal approaches as a deliberate endeavor to conjure the irrational dimension of punishment: law, as discipline and as matter, would serve to master the impulsion of cruelty—logos sublimating hubris. The effort is certainly laudable. Repressive institutions and professions as well as politicians should certainly learn from it. But it falls on the social sciences to break the enchantment of this virtuous circle by explaining why police officers, magistrates, and guards punish as they do, why penal populism prevails over utilitarianism and even moderate retributivism, why punishment is so often in excess not only of the crime it sanctions but of what it is supposed to be.

A blind spot in the definition and the justification remains, however. Indeed the work of the agents involved in repression, the discourse of political leaders, and the surplus of suffering are not uniformly deployed in the social space. They target certain categories and certain territories while sparing others. This is precisely what philosophical and legal theories aiming at defining and justifying punishment tend to mask by presenting it as impartial and fair. We must therefore examine the question of the social distribution of punishment by asking: Who gets punished?

Notes

1. H. L. A. Hart, "The Presidential Address: Prolegomenon to the Principles of Punishment," *Proceedings of the Aristotelian Society* 60 (1959–60): 1–26, esp. 3.

2. Thomas McPherson, "Punishment: Definition and Justification," *Analysis* 28.1 (1967): 21–27.

3. John Rawls, "Two Concepts of Rules," *Philosophical Review* 64.1 (1955): 3–32.

4. Jeremy Bentham, *An Introduction to the Principles of Morals and Legislation* (1780; Oxford: Clarendon Press, 1907), 170–71.

5. Franklin Zimring and Gordon Hawkins, *Incapacitation: Penal Confinement and the Restraint of Crime* (Oxford: Oxford University Press, 1995).

6. Gary Becker, "Crime and Punishment: An Economic Approach," *Journal of Political Economy* 76.2 (1968): 179–217; Annie Kensey and Abdelmalik Benaouda, "Les risques de récidive des sortants de prison: Une nouvelle évaluation," *Cahiers d'études pénitentiaires et criminologiques,* Direction de l'administration pénitentiaire, 36 (2011); Raymond Paternoster, "How Much Do We Really Know about Criminal Deterrence," *Journal of Criminal Law and Criminology* 100.3 (2010): 765–823; Olivier Roeder, Lauren-Brooke Eisen, and Julia Bowling, *What Caused the Crime Decline* (New York: Brennan Center for Justice, 2015).

7. Robert Martinson, "What Works? Questions and Answers about Prison Reform," *Public Interest* 10 (1974): 22–54; Francis Allen, *The Decline of the Rehabilitative Ideal* (New Haven, CT: Yale University Press, 1981); Marc Lipsey and Francis Cullen, "The Effects of Correctional Rehabilitation: A Review of Systematic Reviews," *Annual Review of Law and Social Sciences* 3 (2007): 297–320.

8. Immanuel Kant, *The Philosophy of Law: An Exposition of the Fundamental Principles of Jurisprudence and the Science of Right,* trans. W. Hastie (Edinburgh: T. & T. Clark, 1887; first published in German in 1797), 194–204.

9. Robin Antony Duff, "Penal Communications: Recent Works in the Philosophy of Punishment," *Crime and Justice* 20 (1996): 1–97.

10. Joel Feinberg, "The Expressive Function of Punishment," *The Monist* 49.3 (1965): 397–423.

11. Jean Hampton, "Correcting Harms versus Righting Wrongs: The Goal of Retribution," *UCLA Law Review* 39 (1992): 1659–702.

12. H. J. McCloskey, "A Non-Utilitarian Approach to Punishment," *Inquiry* 8 (1965): 239–55; Gertrude Ezorsky, "The Ethics of Punishment," in *Philosophical Perspectives on Punishment,* ed. Gertrude Ezorsky (Albany: State University of New York, 1972), xi–xxvii.

13. Friedrich Nietzsche, *On the Genealogy of Morals,* trans. Walter Kaufman (New York: Vintage Books, 1989; first published in German in 1887), especially Second essay, section 13.

14. U.S. Department of Justice, "Investigation of the Ferguson Police Department," March 4, 2015, https://www.justice.gov/sites/default/files/opa/press-releases/attachments/2015/03/04/ferguson_police_department_report.pdf.

15. Émile Durkheim, *The Division of Labor in Society,* trans. W. D. Hall (New York: Free Press, 1984; first published in French in 1893), esp. 44 and 47–48.

16. Nietzsche, *On the Genealogy of Morals*, esp. Second essay, section 5.

17. Ashley Lopez, "Allegations of Abuse of Mentally-Ill in Florida Prison," *Miami Herald*, May 21, 2014; Richard Luscombe, "Inmate Locked in Scalding Shower Died 'by Accident,' Medical Examiner Says," *Guardian*, February 27, 2016.

18. Allen Beck, Marcus Berzofsky, Rachel Caspar, and Christopher Krebs, *Sexual Victimization in Prisons and Jails Reported by Inmates 2011–12* (Washington, DC: Bureau of Justice Statistics, 2013).

19. Lisa Guenther, *Solitary Confinement: Social Death and Its Afterlives* (Minneapolis: University of Minnesota Press, 2013); Solitary Watch, "Facts," 2015, http://solitarywatch.com/facts/faq/; Marc Berman, "Albert Woodfox, the Last 'Angola 3' Prisoner, Is Released after More Than 40 Years in Solitary Confinement," *Washington Post*, February 19, 2016; Chelsea Manning, "Solitary Confinement Is 'No Touch' Torture, and Must Be Abolished," *Guardian*, May 2, 2016.

20. Everett Hughes, "Good People and Dirty Work," *Social Problems* 10.1 (1962): 3–11.

21. James Q. Whitman, *Harsh Justice: Criminal Punishment and the Widening Divide between America and Europe* (Oxford: Oxford University Press, 2003); Nicola Lacey, *The Prisoner's Dilemma: Political Economy and Punishment in Contemporary Democracies* (Cambridge, UK: Cambridge University Press, 2008).

22. *To Catch a Predator*, later re-created as *Hansen vs. Predator*. See Spencer Woodman, "Chris Hansen Is Back to Catching Predators," *New Republic*, October 18, 2015; *Lockup 360*, http://www.msnbc.com/lockup.

23. Michel Foucault, *Discipline and Punish: The Birth of the Prison*, trans. Alan Sheridan (New York: Pantheon Books, 1979; first French edition 1975), esp. 3–69; Mona Lynch, "On-line Executions: The Symbolic Use of the Electric Chair in the Cyberspace," *Political and Legal Anthropology Review* 23.2 (2000): 1–20.

24. Kate Shatzkin, "Judges Are Resorting to Shame in Sentencing Criminals," *Los Angeles Times*, April 26, 1998; Dean Murphy, "Justice as Morality Play That Ends with Shame," *New York Times*, June 3, 2001; Jonathan Turley, "Shaming Undermines Justice," *USA Today*, November 17, 2009; Nathaniel Hawthorne, *The Scarlet Letter* (1850; New York: Dover, 1994).

25. Georges Bataille, *The Accursed Share: An Essay on General Economy*, 2 vols. (New York: Zone Books, 1991; first published in French in 1949).

Chapter 3: Who Gets Punished?

Whereas the definition and justification of punishment have fascinated philosophers and jurists, generating substantial literature and rich discussions, its distribution has not received the same attention. Probably the question was hardly one for them since, from their viewpoint, the act of punishing was supposed to be fair, meaning that all offenders—and offenders only—were to be punished on similar principles: a just justice, in sum, which did not call for more theoretical developments.[1] The question: Who gets punished? fell to sociologists and criminologists for its scholarly aspects, and to human rights activists and lawyers for its applied dimension. It is as if the spectacular disparities observed across socioeconomic categories or ethnoracial groups did not make relevant objects for philosophy and law or simply revealed actual differences in the commission of crime. Moreover as both disciplines developed their analyses on the basis of specific situations, whether imagined or real, their casuistry-like reasoning made it difficult to identify systematic differences, which need to be apprehended at a collective level and measured via statistics.

Exceptions to this general observation regarding the relative lack of interest of philosophers and jurists for the unequal distribution of punishment should certainly be mentioned, particularly within the tradition of legal realism and, more recently, critical legal studies. However, the most remarkable but also most atypical of these exceptions is Foucault's work, notably his lectures at the Collège de France on "the punitive society," in which he dedicates a significant part of his reflection to what he calls the "civil war," an unusually dramatic formulation to refer to the eighteenth- and nineteenth-century penal system.[2] This war is a "social war," he writes, a "war of rich against poor," in which the criminal becomes a "social enemy" whose punishment is justified by the fact that he is "someone who wages war on society." Inasmuch as "social laws are made by people for whom they are not intended and applied to those who did not make them," offenses can be differentiated between "popular illegalisms," mostly consisting in depredation, which should be repressed, and "bourgeois illegalisms," principally frauds, which should be spared; the former are seen as an obstacle to the expansion of industrial capitalism, whereas the latter are regarded as its facilitator. Considered from this perspective, the question: Who gets punished? therefore implies another one: What gets punished?, with the latter legitimizing in some way the former. In answering these two interrogations, I will analyze first how the penal system produces a dual differentiation of the offenses and the offenders, and then how this social process is erased, ignored, or disavowed.

The relation between crime and punishment is more equivocal than we commonly presume. Reversing the expected sequence, Durkheim defines crime as "any act which, regardless of degree, provokes against the perpetrator the characteristic reaction known as punishment."[3] And he famously continues, "We must not say that an act offends the common consciousness because it is criminal, but that it is criminal because it offends the common consciousness. We do not condemn it because it is a crime, but it is a crime because we condemn it." Consequently if the acts we call crime depend on social conventions linked to "collective sentiments" according to which we decide what should be punished, then these choices are indicative of moral hierarchies established among human acts. What principle underlies them? asks Durkheim. For instance, why is murder generally deemed the greatest crime in modern society, while an economic crisis or a company's bankruptcy, which may have tragic consequences, including death for many, does not raise similar indignation? The seriousness of the crime therefore does not suffice to explain the disparities observed in its treatment. But Durkheim does not go as far as to wonder whether the hierarchy of the acts may not also reveal a hierarchy of the actors. An element of interpretation of this absence is provided in his later course at the University of Bordeaux recorded by his nephew, in which he opposes "violent crime against persons, that of backward classes and populations," and "soft crime against goods, that of the trading classes and civilized populations."[4] The wording leaves little doubt about his personal predilection.

Probably without having read *The Division of Labor in Society*, two journalists who investigated financial crime in the United States in the aftermath of the 2008 economic crisis reached not so different conclusions. Commenting on nonprosecution agreements reached between the Justice Department and five major banks after seven years of intense negotiations, they wrote: "For most people, pleading guilty to a felony means they will very likely land in prison, lose their job and forfeit their right to vote. But when five of the world's biggest banks plead guilty to an array of antitrust and fraud charges, life will go on, probably without much of a hiccup."[5] In fact, to render the contrast even more striking, they could have added that in the United States, members of disadvantaged categories do not even need to commit a felony to be incarcerated; a minor offense, such as drug possession or traffic violation, suffices. But it would also be interesting to prolong the parallel between mighty bankers and ordinary citizens by comparing, as Durkheim does, the damages caused in terms of the amount of the offenses (dozens of billions of dollars for the frauds vs. several hundred for unpaid fines) and the human consequences of these acts (millions of unemployed people and homeless families due to the crisis vs. no third party wronged by the marijuana user).

During my research in a correctional facility, I had a conversation one afternoon with a twenty-eight-year-old French inmate of Moroccan origin. Living in a housing project with his wife and child, he had worked under multiple short-term contracts until he was arrested for possession and resale of marijuana. Although it was his first conviction, he was sentenced to three years in prison. With a disillusioned smile, he told me that he felt "the injustice of justice." He admitted that he had committed an offense and accepted being punished for it, but he was indignant about the disparities in the retribution of crime: "I was dealing pot. I'm not saying it's not wrong, but it's only marijuana. I never hurt anybody. I never stole from anyone. I never even shoplifted. I pay my taxes and my fines. So, when I see Sarkozy profiting from the riches of a senile old woman or Cahuzac and the millions he owes to the treasury . . . and they're free!" He was referring to the former conservative French president, who was accused of having received clandestine donations from the billionaire Liliane Bettencourt, and the former Socialist minister of budget, who had to resign following the uncovering of his secret bank accounts in Switzerland and Singapore. As a result of long procedures and harsh negotiations, the former had managed to avoid prosecution eight years after the beginning of the investigation, and the latter had obtained a significant reduction of the charge against him.[6] Noticeably the prisoner's observations were validated by official statistics, since in the course of the 2000s, sentences for drug offenses had doubled and those for mere use of marijuana more than tripled, whereas sentences for financial crime had decreased by one-fifth. In the first case, epidemiological studies did not suggest a change in drug consumption: the increase was essentially due to more aggressive repression against users. In the second case, police statistics showed a doubling of the number of offenses: the decline was mostly explained by an official policy of de-penalization of the economic world, with more cases being negotiated.[7] Finally, the man who expressed his bitterness in his cell proved to have a good sociological intuition, analyzing in his own words that one is not sentenced because one is guilty, but one is guilty because one is sentenced. In fact he went even further with this observation as he compared his fate with that of influential and clever politicians, therefore implying that the penal system, relentless toward certain criminals, could be remarkably indulgent with others, whose interests it protected. One could say that he added Marx to Durkheim.

Disparities in the judicial treatment of crime is neither limited to Western society nor specific to the present time. The unequal allocation of punishment is commonly observed in very different contexts. Among the Azande in the north of Democratic Republic of Congo, for instance, punishment traditionally depended on both who was offended and who was the offender.[8] Offenses against a chief were more severely sanctioned than similar offenses against the rest of the group, and symmetrically retribution was harsher on low-ranking offenders than on members of the ruling clan. While "a commoner was liable to punishment for every offense against another commoner or an office-holder," it was unlikely for him "to dare to establish guilt on the part even of the most powerless" of the dominant clan. If one of the latter was accused of witchcraft, the case remained secret, whereas if the same misdeed was suspected among the former, punishment was the only possible outcome. Similarly under the Saadi dynasty in sixteenth-century Fes and Marrakech, the status of the person who had committed a crime decisively influenced the sanction: "a high social rank led to a lighter sentence," and "the punishment displayed the social hierarchy."[9] The difference in treatment was legitimized by a hadith that implied that high-ranking individuals should be forgiven because "for them, reprobation is more painful than physical chastisement." For the most serious crimes, the ultimate sanction of which was death, a high status spared the culprit the humiliation of a public presentation, naked and handcuffed, in the streets of the city before the execution; instead the criminal had his throat cut in prison before his remains were displayed. In modern Europe this differentiation in punishment was visible in the composition of the prison population. At the end of the nineteenth century in the French correctional system, the poor were so closely associated mentally with the carceral world that its material conditions and its meager diet were imagined or, more exactly, justified as a function of their presence.[10] Whether workers, vagrants, or beggars, depending on the economic cycles, they constituted the dangerous classes, whose members were viewed as social predators and sexually promiscuous. They were overrepresented in the jails of the Third Republic with another category: the foreigners, mostly Italians. Carceral demographics thus reflected both crime, with its socioeconomic determinants, and penality, with its moral and judicial prejudices. Many ethnological and historical examples would thereby prove true the moral of La Fontaine's fable "The Animals Sick of the Plague," in which the misdemeanor of the ass is punished by the death of the culprit, while the lion and other powerful animals are exonerated of their egregious crimes: "Thus human courts acquit the strong, / And doom the weak, as therefore wrong." Of these two verses there is another translation: "According as you're feeble, or have might, / High courts condemn you to be black or white."[11] Introducing a symbolic color line, this version seems particularly well adapted to the situation in the United States.

A case in point, its prison system has also been the most studied. It is both exceptional, for the extreme severity of its punitive system and the profound disparities in its distribution, and exemplary, in that it reveals general mechanisms of differentiation in the allocation of punishment. With more than 700 per 100,000 of the national population, the country has the highest incarceration rate in the world, far above Russia and China, thus apparently refuting Montesquieu's statement: "Severity in penalties suits despotic government, whose principle is terror, better than monarchies and republics, which have honor and virtue for their spring. In these states a good legislator will insist less on punishing crimes than on preventing them." The French philosopher added: "It would be easy to prove that in all or nearly all states of Europe penalties have decreased in proportion as one has approached or departed from liberty."[12] Had he lived in the present time, the author of *The Spirit of the Laws* might have revised his analysis so as to account for the paradox of democracies in which liberty and equality are in such tension that the deprivation of the former becomes a major contributor to the failure of the latter. Indeed in no other domain than that of punishment do the two cardinal values of democracy combine so effectively their negative effects. The more severe, the more unfair; this is probably one of the very few sociological laws that resist thorough empirical examination.

As Bruce Western demonstrates, if the incarceration rate in federal and state prisons as well as county jails has increased sixfold during the last three decades of the twentieth century, this evolution has affected blacks, especially among low-income groups, much more than whites.[13] Thus between 1980 and 2000 the proportion of men in prison has grown from 0.7 to 2.1 percent for whites and from 3.0 to 7.9 percent for blacks; among men between twenty and forty, it has swelled from 2.1 to 6.7 percent for whites and from 10.7 to 32.4 percent for blacks; figures for Latinos are situated between those of the other two groups. In other words, the incarceration rate has more or less tripled in each group, but the consequences have been much more dramatic for African American men and to a lesser degree Latinos, notably young adults. The expression *mass imprisonment* reflects both of these phenomena: the unprecedented hardening of the penal system and its focalization on disadvantaged ethnic and racial minorities.[14] With regard to life course, when comparing cohorts of men born in the 1940s and in the 1960s, the risk of having ever been imprisoned when they reach the age of thirty-five has increased from 1.4 to 2.9 percent for whites and from 11.0 to 20.5 percent for blacks; among the latter this risk culminates at 58.9 percent for high school dropouts. If one considers the significant biographical events characterizing the 1960s cohort, white men are ten times more likely to have graduated from college than to have ever been incarcerated, whereas black men are two times less likely to have graduated from college than to have been in jail. For black men, the experience of prison rather than higher education has become the norm.

Is this evolution the mere consequence of a similar growth in the number of offenses, especially among black minorities?[15] Although the expansion of carceral demographics began in a period of increase in crime statistics at the end of the 1970s, the curves of the two phenomena do not coincide, and during the 1990s in particular, the incarceration rate doubles while the crime rate declines by one-third; surveys even show that, for the youth, violent crime and property crime drop faster among blacks than among whites. Moreover, while the war on drugs has fueled mass incarceration, with a tenfold growth for imprisonments in relation to drug crime between 1980 and 2000, the disparities in terms of severity are manifest since blacks are arrested three times more often than whites, although studies show that compared to whites, the prevalence of drug use among blacks is one-fourth lower, the number of drug-related emergency visits two to three times smaller, and, in poor communities, the proportion of drug resellers one-third less. As Western concludes, crime is a major everyday reality in disadvantaged neighborhoods in the United States, but it is a "context" rather than a "cause" of the dual phenomenon of mass incarceration and selective repression of black populations, a context that combines racial tensions following the end of the civil rights movement, restructuring of the economy, and law-and-order policies.

The parallel with the French situation suggests both similarities and differences. During the last decades of the twentieth century, prison demographics in France also grew substantially, albeit at a slower pace, barely doubling, if one dare say.[16] The composition of the carceral population and its evolution over time as well as their correlation with crime rates are, however, not well known, due to the relative scarcity of socioeconomic details and the complete absence of ethnoracial information in penal statistics. The

1999 census nevertheless provides a time-limited but precious insight: half of men in prison are blue-collar workers, and two-thirds have dropped out of school before turning eighteen, whereas these two categories each represent only one-third of the general population. The presence of minorities cannot be measured directly since the recording of such data is illegal, but an indirect estimation can be obtained from the census, which indicates that, when compared to the national population, the fathers of inmates were four times more likely to have been born on the African continent, and twice as many prisoners had spoken a language other than French at home as a child. Whereas one cannot speak of mass imprisonment in France, the carceral expansion is accompanied by a marked socioeconomic and ethnoracial differentiation, men of working-class and immigrant families being overrepresented in correctional facilities.

In the short-stay prison I studied, in particular, half of the eight hundred inmates were unemployed, compared to 10 percent in the general population and 12.5 percent among the inhabitants of the local conurbation; one in two declared no profession, and one in four was a blue-collar worker; 40 percent had dropped out of school, and 40 percent had a vocational degree. Moreover, more than three-fourths belonged to ethnoracial minorities, one-third being black men, mostly from Africa, and another third being Arab men, 85 percent of them French citizens. These proportions were even greater among those younger than thirty, only 16 percent of whom were white. In order to verify that this prison was not an outlier in the correctional system, I compared the local and national prison populations using two proxies: the proportion of nonnationals and, among them, the proportion of African citizens; the figures were almost the same in the two populations, strongly suggesting that the composition of this facility was in no way exceptional. Such an overrepresentation of disadvantaged groups (four times more unemployed than in the local population) and ethnoracial minorities (five in six inmates younger than thirty) definitely calls for an interpretation since one could wonder whether carceral demographics do not simply reflect crime statistics: could it be that there are more poor and unemployed, more blacks and Arabs in prison because they are more involved in criminal activities?

The war on drugs may serve as a good illustration of the logics leading to these figures. It started in France more or less at the same time as in the United States, in a similar context of moral panic, partly in reaction to student protests, musical gatherings, and the dangers of a so-called permissive society. The 1970 law on drug abuse punished all drug-related practices, including mere use, which became an offense involving a maximum of one year in prison. In the next forty years, the number of arrests for drug law violations increased sixtyfold, reaching 160,000 each year, which led to 58,000 convictions, including 14,000 prison sentences. But while the legislator was initially mostly concerned with the trafficking of heroin and cocaine, four decades later mere use represents 86 percent of arrests, 60 percent of convictions, and 33 percent of prison sentences, marijuana being involved in 90 percent of cases.[17] Of the 120,000 incarcerations each year, one in eight is for drug law violations: one-fourth for mere use, but only one-eighth for trafficking. There is thus a double inversion in terms of both harmfulness of the activity (from trafficking to use) and toxicity of the substance (from heroin and cocaine to marijuana). Most of the repression of drug-related offenses in France now focuses on a practice and a product that have been decriminalized in almost all neighboring countries; only Sweden, Finland, and, under specific circumstances, Belgium and Spain (when consumption is collective or public, respectively) penalize marijuana use.[18] One could add that this repression seems ineffective since marijuana consumption has increased considerably in the past decades, France having one of the highest proportions of users in Europe.

The paradox of a repression exercised on the activity and the substance least detrimental to public order and public health, which the state is supposed to protect, should not be a surprise. By targeting an ordinary practice that concerns more than 15 million occasional consumers and 1.5 million regular users, public authorities allow themselves to concentrate this repression on certain categories of the population since it is obviously impossible to arrest all those who smoke cannabis.[19] Although epidemiological surveys show that, among young people, marijuana use is relatively similar across the social spectrum, being slightly higher in the middle class, police work focuses on the youth from disadvantaged neighborhoods and low-income backgrounds. Patrolling takes place in housing projects rather than in the vicinity of universities. Stop-and-frisks affect those who reside in the former rather than those who study in the latter. As I could observe during my fieldwork with the police even when officers noticed that groups of students were ostensibly smoking cannabis in public spaces, their role was not to question or arrest them but to protect them against the potential depredations of which they could be the victims by "project youths" while under the influence. Consequently convictions for drug law violations concern only members of the working class of immigrant origin, who are the only ones to be targeted. Moreover, as offenders are caught red-handed, arrests almost always lead to immediate appearance trials, the prison sentences of which are twice as frequent as in traditional procedures. In these punitive logics, politicians are decisive, not only via the legislation they enact and the decrees they promulgate but also through the instructions they give the police in terms of arrest quotas and the pressure they exert on the judges by demanding inflexibility. Thus from the street where an individual has been found in possession of a small quantity of cannabis to the jail where he enters twenty-four hours later, each step of the penal procedure is influenced by decisions that amount to choosing who must be punished.

The criminalization of marijuana users is often downplayed with the argument that prison sentences are exceptional in relation to the number of arrests. It is true that only one arrest in four leads to a conviction, which, in three-fourths of the cases, is limited to a fine, an educational measure, or an alternative sentence. However, this reasoning eludes two elements that crucially contribute to the social differentiation in penalization. First, for the 135,000 drug users who are arrested, the punishment principally consists of the humiliation of the stop-and-frisk, often in front of friends or relatives, of the mortification of the handcuffing and custody, occasions for abuses, of the lost time and interrupted activities with their academic or professional consequences, with also the risk of a blunder leading to an accusation of insulting the police and resisting arrest. Second, in the end, 3,300 prison sentences are delivered for mere marijuana use and 5,600 for possession of small quantities of cannabis, which represent 7 percent of all prison sentences. Besides, the more than 10,000 suspended sentences with probation for similar charges are both threats of more severe sanctions in case of new infractions and traces left in the criminal record, which jointly compromise the individual's future judicially as well as professionally.[20] Such a close analysis of penal statistics is indispensable to comprehend the real impact of the criminalization of drug use as well as its distribution within society. Retribution cannot be reduced to prison sentencing. Society has many other ways of punishing those it wants to punish. The war on drugs is exemplary in this respect. Indeed the shift of its target not only concerns practices and products; it is also manifest in terms of the publics it sanctions, with working-class youths of color replacing the middle-class white youth of its early years. What this history reveals is that the extension of the definition of illegalisms to be punished allows for a social differentiation of its repression: by displacing the focus from heroin trafficking to marijuana use, one can much better circumscribe the population to sanction, that is, punish essentially those who have been a priori defined as punishable. It is this mechanism that explains why more severity induces more disparity.

To offer a general interpretation of this phenomenon, should we not suppose, then, with Foucault, that "the prison, and no doubt punishment in general, is not intended to eliminate offenses, but rather to distinguish them, to distribute them, to use them; that it is not so much that they render docile those who are liable to transgress the law, but that they tend to assimilate the transgression of the laws in the general tactics of subjection?"[21] The failure of the war on drugs, despite the increasing repression of drug law violations, and its focus on certain publics, which have for corollary to spare others, seems to validate this hypothesis: the prime objective of this policy is not to reduce drug use but to differentiate legally this offense from other offenses and therefore the corresponding offenders from other offenders.[22] It is, indeed, by selecting the crime to be punished and by determining among criminals which ones should be targeted that the penal system can better distinguish populations—focusing on marijuana use rather than embezzlement cases, patrolling housing projects rather than residential areas. Selective repression of certain illegalisms and social groups therefore plays a major role in the production and reproduction of social disparities. But how does this distribution of penalties operate, and how can we explain why it is ultimately so well tolerated socially? These are the two questions that we now have to address.

In that regard, criminal courts can be viewed as sites par excellence of diffraction of the social through the prism of the penal. In one of the immediate appearance trials I attended, a nineteen-year-old man is charged for "having violently resisted" three police officers during a stop-and-frisk and for "having insulted them via words, gestures and menaces" while in custody at the precinct. A French citizen born of Senegalese parents, he lives in a city renowned for having hosted, in the middle of the twentieth century, one of the first public housing projects, intended mostly for the population from former colonies. Two-thirds of the youth of the city are of non-European origin—three times more than the national average. One-third of households live under the poverty threshold, and one youth in four is unemployed; for both indicators, this is twice the regional average. The accused resides with his mother, who alone raises her five children in one of the three projects administratively classified as "sensitive urban zones" due to a combination of unfavorable social indicators. He has dropped out of high school, begun a vocational degree, and unsuccessfully gone on the job market. His criminal record already contains five summonses, including one other accusation of insulting the police and resisting arrest, which makes him the ideal usual suspect. As his mother later explains to me, he is constantly harassed by law enforcement agents, who stop and frisk him without reason, and he has recently been arrested and kept in custody twice for offenses that were subsequently discovered to have been committed by others. During the immediate appearance trial, obviously shaken by his stay in the police cell and ill at ease in the tribunal but not wanting to lose face, the young man answers awkwardly and abruptly the questions of the judge, who expresses his irritation. The earlier encounter with the state-appointed lawyer did not go well, and the speech for the defense lacks conviction. After a brief deliberation, the judge announces that, one officer being absent from the trial because he was not summoned on time, the trial is adjourned, but that, in the interval, the accused must be held in remand for lack of guarantee that he will not reiterate his offense and that he will appear in court in due time. As his mother implores the judge to release him until the court date, he is handcuffed and taken to the local jail, while the two officers present at the hearing leave the room, visibly satisfied.

Although remand is supposed to be "a last resort" option decided "on exceptional grounds" when a probation measure or a house arrest is impossible, it concerns fifteen thousand people in immediate appearance trials, that is, one-third of these lawsuits and, on the whole, one incarceration in five in France.[23] Moreover, when the case is later heard, it is almost always followed by a prison sentence, the duration of which corresponds at least to the time spent in remand. Thus even if remand is technically a preventive measure, it also entails a punitive component. Insulting the police and resisting arrest, which is the charge against the young man, represents fifteen thousand sentences each year, one-third of them involving imprisonment. Considering that the present case was a repeat offense, such a sentence appeared all the more likely since in the absence of witnesses it was the word of a sworn officer against the word of a project youth. To anticipate the final decision by choosing the remand was therefore logical from the point of view of the judge, which rendered his juridical arguments somewhat rhetorical. In such a situation the accused is presumed guilty on the basis of his antecedents and his attitude. The prison sentence will later confirm his guilt.

There is no doubt that the behavior of the suspect in the tribunal adds to the negative impression that his criminal record produces. It proceeds from both the habitus of his milieu and his ignorance of justice codes: by arrogance as much as clumsiness, he successively alienates his attorney and the judge; by pride as much as inexperience, he does not want or does not know how to make amends. Through his conduct he thus comforts the prejudices betrayed by the magistrates' insinuations, their condescending tone, and their contemptuous remarks in an aside. Finally, the verdict has more to do with what he is than what he is accused of having done. Or more accurately: one judges what he is supposed to have done in light of who one thinks he is. It is also in this way that police practices that have led to the incident of which he is accused can be interpreted. In his neighborhood, law enforcement agents know him too well. If a misdemeanor or a crime occurs, the presumption of guilt prevails, as in the two occasions when he was arrested, kept in custody, and released after the actual culprit was identified. If he is present in a public space, he is submitted to various forms of subjection, without the habitual legal justifications or precautions, as during his recent encounter. Stop-and-frisks, insults, and abuses serve at least to inflict a punishment on the spot, even to generate a conflictive situation that may lead to a legal sanction as well. Certain officers do not dissimulate their intentions; regarding individuals whom they consider to have been insufficiently punished, they say that they will have "their suspended prison sentence revoked." The concerned youths do not ignore the threat; once they have had dealings with the police, they know that the only way to escape their bullying is to "leave the hood." But the judges do not seem aware of this modus operandi of the public forces. They stick to the version of the sworn agents and get annoyed by the protests of these young men whom they deem rough.

To understand the case involving the young man of Senegalese origin, they would have to take into account the social conditions of possibility of his criminal record. These can be analyzed at a dual level: structural (life in a difficult neighborhood) and circumstantial (interactions with the police), the two being closely linked in his everyday experience. On the one hand, the offenses of which the suspect has been found guilty in the past, notably the thefts, are offenses facilitated by the social environment where he grew up, with its economic precarity, the lack of professional prospects, the existence of unlawful opportunities, and the access to criminal networks.[24] As Foucault observed about the illegalisms of another time, depredation is typical of certain low-income classes in the same way as fraud is characteristic of certain wealthy milieux. On the other hand, this time the accusation that brings the young man before a judge is for an alleged offense during a stop-and-frisk. But this sort of police activity is not distributed at random. Law enforcement agents target certain territories and certain populations, and this focus has less to do with the incidence of crime than with logics of control and performance that determine practices that would hardly be imaginable in other places and with other categories: in disadvantaged neighborhoods, stop-and-frisks mostly serve to impose and manifest a social order; they are meant to "remind these people of their place" in society, and more specifically to remind them that they are "police properties."[25] In Foucault's terms, what is at stake is the subjection of these populations. Thus structural factors enlighten past illicit activity as much as circumstantial elements illuminate the present accusation. However, to invoke the social conditions of possibility in the interpretation of a criminal case implies neither determinism (most people living in a disadvantaged milieu do not engage in unlawful practices, and most youths exposed to police harassment do not react to their bullying) nor justification (the point is not a moral assessment). It means to find ways to understand what went on and why; in other words, for the judges, it means to make informed decisions about the cases they have to adjudicate.

Yet most of the time justice ignores these conditions. And what magistrates perceive of them often works against the defendants belonging to low-income classes, especially those of immigrant origin, on two counts, as is clear in the present case. First, the social representation that the judge has of the young man's milieu increases his suspicion: the image of the housing project supports the criminal record and the current offense rather than rendering them intelligible. Second, the social competences that the young man is able to mobilize in court are completely at odds with the norms and expectations of the magistrates; by his attitude he antagonizes them but also lets them think that he probably behaved in the same way with the police. Sociological studies have long established that this dual causality—the judges' social representations and the defendants' social competences—accounts for the considerable disparities observed in court decisions.[26] Here, the disparities and the logics that explain them become even more obvious if we contrast the case of the young man of Senegalese origin with another one, heard the same day.

Minutes later a student accused of having abused and raped his partner appears before the court. The facts seem to have been easily established as, on the one hand, a physician has certified the genital wounds caused by the penetration and given the young woman six-day temporary disability, and on the other hand, a previous aggression had sent the young woman to the emergency room due to the fracture of a finger bone for which she had nevertheless filed no complaint. The middle-class male student, who is of French origin, lives in a residential town. He expresses himself well, adopts a humble posture, admits having been violent, but denies the sexual abuses, manifests his regrets, and promises to change his ways. The judge, whose son, also a student, attends the hearing with two friends, seems less impatient than in the previous case. The lawyer, who is remunerated by the young man's parents, is unusually verbose in her defense plea. The hearing lasts twice as long as the average in immediate appearance trials. When the verdict, a six-month suspended prison sentence, is publicly delivered, the student's family loudly celebrates, while the victim, alone on her bench, looks completely overwhelmed.

Thus, whereas the young black man from a disadvantaged environment accused of having talked back to the police and hindered his arrest as he was once more subjected to an unjustified stop-and-frisk is sent to jail, the white middle-class student accused of repeated physical abuse and rape goes home with his parents. It is worth noting that, under the French law, the offenses of insulting the police and resisting arrest are punished with a maximum of six and twelve months in jail, respectively, while individuals convicted of sexual violence incur a five-year prison sentence, extended to fifteen years if a rape has been committed and even more if it has caused wounds, as in the present case. Surprising with respect to the statutory sanctions, the difference in treatment between the two cases is, however, not so difficult to comprehend when taking into account the distance between the social worlds of the defendants and the disparity of their social competences in court, two elements that, subjectively, lead the judge to feel animosity against one and show leniency toward the other and, objectively, weigh on both the assessment of the offense and the estimation of the risk of recidivism. The objectivation of the decision in legal language allows eluding the subjective aspect of social affinities, the judge being convinced that he has ruled impartially for the common good.

Social inequality is therefore doubly overlooked: in the conditions underlying the criminal record and in the circumstances of the adjudication of the case. This ignorance of the social dimension of both the alleged offense and the judicial decision has for corollary two principles of modern legal theory, especially in the French context: the liability of the offender and the individualization of the sanction. Both are intricately linked. Establishing the liability of the offender is necessary to justify legally the sanction against him, while reciprocally the individualization of the sanction supposes that the corresponding individual be liable. One has to decide whether the person has committed the act of which he is accused as well as whether he can be held liable for it with regard to his intention, his mental health, his not being coerced, in other words *actus reus* and *mens rea*. But the question of liability exceeds the legal frame; it includes a moral dimension of accountability toward oneself and others, a psychological dimension of culpability, which implies accepting the guilt for the act committed, and a philosophical dimension of responsibility, which brings free will and determinism in tension. Cornerstone of the punishment, the liability does not take into account the structural and circumstantial parts of the alleged offense, as defined earlier. But although it is supposed to apprehend the personal situation of the defendant, the individualization of the sanction, as it is implemented in tribunals, tends to accentuate the disparities in judicial decisions, not only because, by definition, it singularizes the cases but also because most of the elements of the social context tend to become incriminating evidence. In particular, the so-called quick social investigation, which complements the criminal record and the police report, is mostly used to anticipate the risk of recidivism or, if the trial is adjourned, the necessity of a remand, instead of providing mitigating circumstances in relation to a troubled family history or difficult living conditions, for instance. Adding to the negative self-presentation in court, these elements penalize the defendants belonging to disadvantaged and stigmatized categories. In immediate appearance trials, most of them end up in jail either after a prison sentence has been delivered or after a remand has been decided before the trial. Both the liability of the offender and the individualization of the sanction therefore contribute to a narrowing of retribution on the individual held liable, who is deemed solely accountable for the act he allegedly committed and those he might commit in the future.

But has it always and everywhere been the case? The answer offered by Nietzsche is clear: "The idea, now so obvious, apparently so natural, even unavoidable, that had to serve as the explanation of how the sense of justice ever appeared on earth—'the criminal deserves to be punished because he could have acted differently'—is in fact an extremely late and subtle form of human judgment and inference." Indeed "throughout the greater part of human history punishment was not imposed because one held the wrongdoer responsible for his deed, thus not on the presupposition that only the guilty one should be punished."[27] Punishment, when it took place, was an emotional reaction against the perpetrator of a crime, but this "anger" was moderated by "the idea that every injury has its equivalent and can actually be paid back." In ancient or remote societies in which, as we have seen, the expectation of a reparation prevailed over the infliction of a pain, the question of liability was not relevant for the individual or for the group. As E. E. Evans-Pritchard writes, whereas in the past the whole clan contributed to the payment of the debt thus incurred, it was "not in virtue of collective responsibility, but in virtue of social obligations to a kinsman." Colonization introduced the principle, so foreign to the traditional world, of individual liability, which has for implication that "today if a man kills a person by witchcraft, the crime is his sole responsibility, and his kin are not associated with his guilt."[28] It should be added that in these societies, witchcraft does not necessarily involve malevolence, but is often a fate endured by the witch: it is an evil force that can act independently of the agent's will, who is therefore not considered to be guilty. The ethnological detour thus suggests that there is no necessary or universal relationship between the acknowledgment of the causality linking an act and an agent and the idea of responsibility as we understand it. The latter developed historically independent of the former. It is a cultural fact, the evolution of which can be followed in philosophical debates and juridical texts.

By confronting the individual with his act under the exclusive principle of liability, society absolves itself of its responsibility in the social production and construction of illegalisms, if we call social production the way contexts and situations facilitate them and social construction the manner in which they are distinguished and punished. That the distribution of wealth, resources, and populations in the social space partakes of a differentiation of offenses, that the selective identification and sanction of these offenses participates in the unequal allocation of penalties, and finally that these processes circumscribe what is condemnable and who is punishable is not only ignored but also disavowed. In recent years it has even become customary to denounce those who formulate these elementary social facts. In France the analysis of the social processes underlying crime has been assimilated with a search for "sociological excuses" by two prime ministers, whereas in the United States it has been deemed an "insidious trend," which is part of the problem itself, by two former presidents.[29] Social scientists are thus accused of contributing to the disorders they study. To try to understand is already to justify: thus goes the common political discourse across the ideological spectrum. This accusation offers a dual advantage for those in power: it eludes their social accountability and legitimizes their punitive policies.

This discourse is all the more remarkable since it is expressed in a period of deepening socioeconomic inequalities—a phenomenon prevalent across the Western world. In the United States, where it began in the 1970s, income growth has been 37 percent for the bottom 20 percent and 187 percent for the top 1 percent between 1979 and 2013.[30] During the same period the prison population multiplied by five and the crime rate dropped by one-third. In France, where the gap started to widen in the 1990s, the average income has decreased by 6.2 percent for the bottom decile, while it augmented by 11.8 percent for the top decile between 2002 and

2012, the ratio between the two growing from 6.0 to 7.2.[31] During the same decade the carceral demographics swelled by 52 percent, whereas homicides continued their decline. Apart from their temporality and intensity, the trends are thus similar in both countries. Loïc Wacquant depicts the experience of the United States as a "living laboratory of the neoliberal future" of France and, more broadly, Europe.[32] The efforts deployed to reject any attempt to link these phenomena are all the more troubling. How can we comprehend that at the very moment when social insecurity increases, crime wanes, and prisons fill, criticisms against social analysis and emphasis on individual liability become so preeminent?

To use a psychoanalytical concept, one might speak of disavowal, that is, the rejection of a reality that would be unbearable to admit.[33] If indeed it appeared that one punishes more and more independently of the evolution of crime, that one penalizes offenses less on the basis of their gravity than according to those who commit them, that one criminalizes selectively the most socioeconomically vulnerable and the most ethnoracially marginalized populations, and finally that this whole process makes society less safe in the short term and more divided in the long run, then one can guess how much this revelation would be intolerable to contemporary democracies. Conversely, to consider that everyone is individually liable for his acts, that all sentences delivered under the law are just deserts, and that the penal system thus protects the safety of the nation is both acceptable and comforting. From a moral perspective, the second version is definitely more rewarding than the first. But my intention in incorporating a psychoanalytic idea should not be misunderstood: I am not trying to apply to social contradictions a concept meant to interpret psychic conflicts. There is no more Freudian social unconscious than there is Durkheimian collective consciousness.

In resorting to this vocabulary I simply want to suggest that a substantial proportion of the people who think about crime and punishment from the idealistic and punitive perspective of the second version rather than in the realistic and troubling terms of the first are sincere in their belief in what they deem a just order. As far as politicians are concerned, in contrast, I am less persuaded that they honestly defend these ideas and I would be tempted, for most of them, to analyze their posture in the language of Sartre's bad faith or as a lack of Foucault's courage of truth since, although they have access to all the elements necessary to apprehend these difficult issues in a rational way, they prefer to use them instrumentally for electoral purposes. This is certainly a crucial key to the success of penal populism: the encounter between genuine concern for security and tactical manipulation of constituencies, between supposed common sense and well-understood interest, between conviction and cynicism, all elements the boundaries of which remain uncertain and shifting but which have in common to elude a dispassionate confrontation with and rigorous interpretation of facts. The resulting gap between the real world and its biased representation corresponds to what Bernard Harcourt, in his analysis of the particular example of the successful "broken windows theory," calls an "illusion."[34] In the present case, the contemporary punitive illusion resides in the gap between the ideal of fair punishment that is asserted and the reality of the unequal distribution of retribution that one refuses to see.

A striking illustration of this gap is the extension of the domain of punishment far beyond its expected perimeter, that is, the retribution of the convict as formulated in the sentence. The inclusion of a greater number of individuals in the penal demographics and the hardening of sanctions against them has consequences that exceed the mere execution of the sanction at two levels: on the offenders themselves and on their families and more broadly their communities. The convict, especially when sentenced to jail, often loses his job, has a hard time finding another one, and gets excluded from certain professions or activities; if a foreigner, he is confronted with problems renewing his residence permit or obtaining citizenship, and can even be deported; in the United States he may be deprived of his right to welfare and public housing and even of his right to vote, disenfranchisement for felony offenses affecting almost six million people, mostly poor African Americans.[35] But his family also bears the burden of the punishment, particularly when there is a prison sentence, which implies the loss of what was often the main source of income, the accumulation of administrative and financial complications, the cost of visits to the correctional facility; for partners, the emotional tensions of present hardships and an uncertain future add to the multiplication of tasks and responsibilities regarding the household and the increased personal dependence toward relatives, as they may have to move back into their parents' home; for children, the absence of fatherly authority and the destructuring of the family frequently result in psychological issues, high dropout rates, and potentially juvenile delinquency; in the United States neighborhoods affected by mass incarceration are more exposed to urban violence and illicit economies.[36] Thus, in successive circles, whole segments of society become afflicted by the deleterious effects of punitive policies.

On July 16, 2015, at the end of what appears to have been the first visit of a president of the United States to a correctional facility, Barack Obama gave a brief improvised talk in front of the staff and journalists. To a question asking what had impressed him the most during this visit, he replied that it was his conversation with a small group of inmates: "When they describe their youth and their childhood, these are young people who made mistakes that are not that different from the mistakes I made and the mistakes a lot of you made. The difference is they did not have the kinds of support structures, the second chances, the resources that would allow them to survive those mistakes." He continued saying that it was normal for adolescents to make mistakes, but what was not normal was that so many of them would end up in prison. He concluded, "That's what strikes me—there but for the grace of God."[37] This remarkable sentence goes beyond the mere acknowledgment of the social injustice that underlies punitive practices. It undermines what is perhaps the most invisible foundation of punishment, namely the relationship of otherness that it presumes. Between the one who is judged and the one who judges him, whether a magistrate, an officer, a politician, or an ordinary citizen, a radical distance is instituted, which is always moral since there is an offense or a crime, but is also frequently social, when the suspect is from another milieu or origin. This otherization, so to speak, is what allows condescension, inflexibility, and even, sometimes, cruelty. It is what allows a punitive society. The president's epiphany during his visit at the prison suddenly questioned this prejudice and opened the possibility of reflecting on the inequality in the allocation of punishment.

Most normative theories of punishment ignore the question of its implementation and more specifically of its distribution. It is as if a veil of ignorance allowed the legislator and the judge to decide which infractions to sanction and what sentence to deliver, independently of prejudices or interests. The decision being fair, its application is assumed to be proportionate to the crime and its allocation equitable among criminals. However, empirical studies unsurprisingly reveal a huge gap between what should be and what is. These variations are not anecdotal or individual; they not only reflect representatives' moods or judges' characters. They reveal systematic and convergent trends. Statistical data establish their regularity. Ethnographic observation illuminates their comprehension.

The delimitation of the acts considered to be offenses and of the offenses deemed penalized is determined not only by the gravity of these acts but by the publics to be punished. This differentiation of offenses and offenders increases when repression hardens. The intensification of the punitive pressure is accompanied by a widening of the spectrum of the acts to be sanctioned, which leads to an expansion of the total number of people penalized as well as a concentration of the repression on certain publics. But punishment is not limited to the sentence and the convict. It extends beyond prison time and affects family and friends. Consequently, punishable populations are defined not only in terms of those who are convicted of crimes but also by default and in excess: on the one hand, by the exclusion of guilty people whom the authorities want to spare the opprobrium of the punishment and, on the other hand, by the inclusion of innocent people whom the power punishes via the contamination of another's conviction. The distribution of punishment therefore participates in the aggravation and perpetuation of social disparities by disproportionately affecting the most disadvantaged segments of the population, whose present conditions are often the legacy of particular historical circumstances such as slavery, colonization, or immigration. This means that the question of punishment cannot only proceed from an idealistic theory of justice. It must also be inscribed in a realistic theory of equality holding societies accountable for both their past and their present.

Notes

1. H. L. A. Hart, "The Presidential Address: Prolegomenon to the Principles of Punishment," *Proceedings of the Aristotelian Society* 60 (1959–60): 1–26, esp. 10–12.

2. Michel Foucault, *The Punitive Society: Lectures at the Collège de France 1972–1973*, trans. Graham Burchell (New York: Palgrave-MacMillan, 2015; first published in French 2013), esp. the January 10, 1973, and February 21, 1973, lectures.

3. Émile Durkheim, *The Division of Labor in Society*, trans. W. D. Hall (New York: Free Press, 1984; first published in French in 1893), esp. 31–33.

4. Marcel Mauss, "In memoriam: L'œuvre inédite de Durkheim et de ses collaborateurs," in *Oeuvres 3: Cohésion sociale et divisions de la sociologie* (1925; Paris: Minuit, 1969), 473–567.

5. Ben Protess and Michael Corkery, "Five Big Banks Expected to Plead Guilty to Felony Charges, but Punishment May Be Tempered," *New York Times*, May 13, 2015; Shaila Dewan, "Probation May Sound Light, but Punishments Can Land Hard," *New York Times*, August 2, 2015.

6. Samuel Laurent, "Si vous n'avez rien suivi à l'affaire Bettencourt," *Le Monde*, January 20, 2015; Renaud Lecadre, "Pourquoi le procès Cahuzac est reporté à septembre?," *Libération*, February 10, 2016.

7. Odile Timbart, "Vingt ans de condamnations pour crimes et délits," *Infostat Justice* 114 (2011); Thierry Godechot, "La délinquance économique et financière serait-elle en voie de disparition?," Délinquance, justice et autres questions de société, November 5, 2010, http://www.laurent-mucchielli.org/public/La_delinquance_economique_et_financiere.pdf.

8. Josef Kandert, "Zande," in *The Early State*, ed. Henri Claessen (The Hague: Mouton, 1978), 511–29, esp. 522.

9. Fernando Rodríguez Medrano, "Justice, crime et châtiment au Maroc au 16e siècle," *Annales Histoire Sciences Sociales* 3 (1996): 611–27.

10. Michelle Perrot, "Délinquance et système pénitentiaire en France au 19e siècle," *Annales: Économies, Sociétés, Civilisations* 30 (1975): 67–91.

11. Jean de La Fontaine, "Les animaux malades de la peste," trans. Elizur Wright and Robert Thomson, in *Fables*, book 7 (1678; Paris: Hachette, 1866).

12. Montesquieu, *The Spirit of the Laws*, trans. Anne Cohler, Basia Miller, and Harold Stone (Cambridge, UK: Cambridge University Press, 1989; first French edition 1748), esp. part 1, chapter 9.

13. Bruce Western, *Punishment and Inequality in America* (New York: Russell Sage Foundation, 2006), pp. 11–33.

14. David Garland, "The Meaning of Mass Imprisonment," in *Mass Imprisonment: Social Causes and Consequences*, ed. David Garland (London: Sage, 2001), 1–3.

15. Western, *Punishment and Inequality in America*, esp. 34–51.

16. Annie Kensey, "Dix ans d'évolution du nombre de personnes écrouées de 2000 à 2010," *Cahiers d'études pénitentiaires et criminologiques*, Direction de l'administration pénitentiaire, 35 (2010); Institut national de la statistique et des études économiques, "L'Histoire familiale des hommes détenus," *Synthèses*, January 2002.

17. Ivana Obradovic, "La pénalisation de l'usage des stupéfiants en France au miroir des statistiques administratives: Enjeux et controverses," *Déviance et Société* 36.4 (2012): 441–69; Odile Timbard and Faustine Busch, *Les Condamnations: Année 2014*, Ministère de la Justice, December 2015, http://www.justice.gouv.fr/art_pix/stat_condamnations_2014.pdf.

18. Toute l'Europe, "Les législations sur le cannabis en Europe," June 11, 2015, http://www.touteleurope.eu/actualite/les-legislations-sur-le-cannabis-en-europe.html.

19. François Beck, Jean-Baptiste Richard, Romain Guignard, Olivier Le Nézet, and Stanislas Spilka, "Les niveaux d'usage des drogues en France en 2014," *Tendances*, OFDT-INPES, 99 (2015).

20. Timbard and Busch, *Les Condamnations*.

21. Michel Foucault, *Discipline and Punish: The Birth of the Prison*, trans. Alan Sheridan (New York: Pantheon Books, 1979; first French edition 1975), esp. 272.

22. John Hagan, *Who Are the Criminals? The Politics of Crime Policy from the Age of Roosevelt to the Age of Reagan* (Princeton, NJ: Princeton University Press, 2010).

23. Commission de suivi de la détention provisoire, *Rapport Annuel 2013*, Ministère de la Justice, http://www.justice.gouv.fr/art_pix/rapport_csdp_2013.pdf.

24. Elijah Anderson, *Codes of the Street: Decency, Violence, and the Moral Life in the Inner City* (New York: Norton, 1999); Alice Goffman, *On the Run: Fugitive Life in an American City* (Chicago: University of Chicago Press, 2014).

25. Richard Ericson, *Reproducing Order: A Study of Police Patrol Work* (Toronto: University of Toronto Press, 1982); John Alan Lee, "Some Structural Aspects of Police Deviance in Relation to Minority Groups," *Organizational Police Deviance: Its Structure and Control*, ed. Clifford Shearing (Scarborough, UK: Butterworth, 1981), 49–82.

26. Aaron Cicourel, *The Social Organization of Juvenile Justice* (New York: Wiley, 1967); Mark Galanter, "Why the 'Haves' Come Out Ahead: Speculations on the Limits of Legal Change," *Law and Society Review* 9.1 (1974): 95–160.

27. Friedrich Nietzsche, *On the Genealogy of Morals*, trans. Walter Kaufman (New York: Vintage Books, 1989; first published in German in 1887), especially Second essay, sections 4, 5, and 6.

28. E. E. Evans-Pritchard, *Witchcraft, Oracles, and Magic among the Azande* (1937; Oxford: Clarendon Press, 1976), esp. 5.

29. Lionel Jospin and Manuel Valls; Ronald Reagan and George H. Bush, in http://www.homme-moderne.org/societe/socio/wacquant/excuses.html.

30. Chad Stone, Dani Trisi, Arloc Sherman, and Emily Horton, *A Guide to Statistics on Historical Trends in Income Inequality* (Washington, DC: Center on Budget and Policy Priorities, 2016).

31. Thomas Piketty, *Capital in the Twenty-First Century*, trans. Arthur Goldhammer (Cambridge, MA: Harvard University Press, 2014; first published in French in 2013); Observatoire des inégalités, "Depuis 15 ans, les inégalités de revenus augmentent," April 22, 2015.

32. Loïc Wacquant, *Punishing the Poor: The Neoliberal Government of Social Insecurity* (Durham, NC: Duke University Press, 2009; first French edition 2004), esp. prologue.

33. Jean Laplanche and Jean-Bertrand Pontalis, *The Language of Psychoanalysis*, trans. Donald Nicholson-Smith (London: Karnak Books, 1988; first published in French in 1967), esp. 118.

34. Bernard Harcourt, *Illusion of Order: The False Promise of Broken Windows Policing* (Cambridge, MA: Harvard University Press, 2001).

35. Michelle Alexander, *The New Jim Crow: Mass Incarceration in the Age of Colorblindness* (New York: New Press, 2010); Marie Gottschalk, *Caught: The Prison State and the Lockdown of American Politics* (Princeton, NJ: Princeton University Press, 2015).

36. Megan Comfort, "Punishment Beyond the Legal Offender," *Annual Review of Law and Social Science* 3 (2007): 271–96; Jeffrey Morenoff and David Hardin, "Incarceration, Prisoner Reentry, and Communities," *Annual Review of Sociology* 40 (2014): 411–29.

37. The White House, "Remarks by the President after Visit at El Reno Federal Correctional Institution," July 16, 2015, https://www.whitehouse.gov/the-press-office/2015/07/16/remarks-president-after-visit-el-reno-federal-correctional-institution.

Conclusion: Rethinking Punishment

"To an observer belonging to a different society, certain practices of ours would appear to be similar in nature to anthropophagy, which we deem so alien to our notion of civilization. I am thinking of our customs regarding justice and prison." Thus writes Claude Lévi-Strauss in a famous passage of *Tristes tropiques*.[1] If such an observer, he continues, were to consider the solution consisting in dealing with dangerous individuals by "expelling them out of the social body and keeping them temporarily or definitively isolated from the rest of humanity, in establishments specially intended for this purpose," most of those "we call primitive would regard such a custom with profound horror," marking us "in their eyes with the same barbarity which we are tempted to impute to them." Taking the example of the Plains Indians, he notes that "it would never have occurred to them that the punishment of the culprit could have implied the rupture of social ties." On the contrary, the settlement of the case involved a reciprocal system of "debt" and "gifts" until obtaining the progressive correction of the disorder. This text was published in 1955, at a time when the French prison population was at its lowest level.

Certainly Lévi-Strauss's critique of the inhumaneness of our justice system might have been even more severe had he been writing six decades later, when the number of inmates has more than tripled in France and been multiplied by 8 in the United States. And to shake our moral assurance, he would perhaps have imagined his fictitious observer wondering which is the cruelest treatment one can apply against one's enemies: their videotaped beheading, usually deemed the ultimate form of barbarity, or their secret indefinite detention, with beatings, waterboarding, sexual abuse, sleep deprivation, forced feeding, exposure to loud music and extreme temperatures? In order to justify his audacious parallel, he might even have called his readers' attention to the fact that the execution of prisoners in the first context was showcased as a macabre parody of torture practices in the second, the victims ironically wearing the same orange jumpsuit. Yet Lévi-Strauss was not a provocateur. An heir of the Enlightenment who affirmed that he would have preferred to live in the nineteenth century, he thought that cultural relativism was not contradictory with ethical universalism, and that anthropology could be of some utility for his contemporaries by questioning their prejudices with regard to other societies and their certainties about their own values. Challenging our self-evidence about punishment, inquiring into the value of our values and the decline of our morality, as Nietzsche has it,[2] is what I have tried to do by revisiting the legal theories that define and justify punishment and by exploring certain social aspects that have been little studied.

Let us summarize the main conclusions of this inquiry. First, the generally admitted link between crime and punishment has many exceptions: not all crimes are deemed deserving of punishment, and not all punishments sanction a crime or suspicion of a crime. Second, the alleged distinction between revenge and punishment often proves difficult to validate empirically; it appears rather as a rhetorical argument used to delegitimize or legitimize certain acts or decisions. Third, the infliction of suffering or of an equivalent form of penalty, which is considered the very essence of punishment, has not always existed; it is the result of a historical shift from an affective economy of the debt to a moral economy of punishment and from a logic of compensation for the damage caused to a rationale of retribution for the wrong done. Fourth, the classic alternative between utilitarianism and retributivism in the justification of punishment pertains to an ideal realm rather than to the actual world; in real-life situations, the justifications provided by the social agents and the interpretations elaborated from an outsider's perspective suggest subjective and objective reasons that are diverse, complex, and remote from the model. Fifth, the rational approach developed by normative disciplines as well as the social sciences leave unexplored an emotional dimension; the indignation regarding the offense and the pleasure in the retribution constitute the obscure and eclipsed part of punishment. Sixth, the social distribution of punishment proceeds from a dual mechanism that, through the law, differentiates offenses according to the supposed social qualities of the offenders and, in court, differentiates sentences according to the social qualities of the supposed offenders; as much as acts amenable to be penalized, one thus distinguishes social groups destined to be punished and others meant to be spared, the allocation of retribution thus reflecting and consolidating social disparities. Seventh, the assertion of the individual liability in the commission of offenses, which goes with the disavowal of their social determinants and circumstances, increasingly prevails as inequality deepens: the more social processes weigh on the production of crime, the less they are recognized as such by judges, politicians, and, ultimately, society.

These proposals, drawn from genealogical and ethnographic material, should certainly be refined or modulated. Yet they provide a framework for a critical approach to the meaning and place of punishment in contemporary societies by putting to the test some basic assertions in moral philosophy and legal studies. Whereas these classical readings have been crucial for the establishment of normative grounds for the definition and justification of punishment and, to a lesser degree, its distribution, there is undoubtedly a risk—intellectual as much as political—in being satisfied with a situation in which ideal punitive forms would never be confronted with their actual expressions and would even contribute to rendering them invisible or unthinkable. If we accept a definition without acknowledging that it overlooks an essential part of the reality of the phenomenon it is supposed to circumscribe; if we concur with justifications without recognizing how little they are in fact mobilized in the public debate, the elaboration of the legislation, and the decisions of the judges; and if we content ourselves with the affirmation that the law is the same for all without understanding that actual inequality in the distribution of penalties and sentences calls for a specific theoretical endeavor; then we can definitely worry that a potentially progressive normative approach supposed to establish the rules of fair punishment will be transformed into a conservative defense of a legal, moral, and, in the end, social order.

The alternative interpretation proposed in these lectures consists, on the contrary, in questioning the foundations of punishment: how it is defined, justified, and distributed—and correlatively whence it comes, how it is inflicted, for what crime, and to which criminals. This approach relies on an empirical investigation but leads to theoretical proposals. One could think that these proposals are remote from current preoccupations, from the anxieties and expectations of the population, from the challenges politicians are facing, from situations the police and judges are confronted with—and from the urgency of the present punitive moment.

In that regard one can easily anticipate the triple accusation of irenicism, elitism, and inconsistency that can be addressed to the critical approach I defend here—and for that matter, to any critical theory. According to its denigrators, this approach would ignore the seriousness of the problem of crime in the contemporary world, its negative effects on society, notably the victims, and the need for public authorities to bring effective solutions; it would also imply a superiority of and priority to intellectual work over the popular demand, as expressed in opinion polls, for more safety, more severity from the legislator, more inflexibility from the judges, and more harshness in the application of sentences; finally, it would comfortably spare the critic the complication of having to say what should be concretely done to reform the penal system while reducing crime rates.

To each of these reservations I want to offer a brief response. First, a critical theory of punishment does not underestimate the reality of crime and the disorders it generates. It invites a reflection, however, on what is considered an offense, why certain acts are tolerated while others are sanctioned, independently of their implications for the common good, and what consequences may have an indefinite extension of the spectrum of punishable acts, especially when it actually delimits the circle of punishable populations. Second, a critical theory of punishment does not overlook the expectations of citizens in the decisions that concern them. It nonetheless considers that invoking public opinion on the basis of methodologically arguable and event-dependent techniques mostly serves to justify and encourage penal populism rather than promotes democratic choice. Third, a critical theory of punishment neither eludes nor disqualifies its translation into action and therefore the need for normative stances. It nevertheless implies that the questioning of what is generally taken for granted, even against the evidence of facts, be an indispensable prerequisite to any discussion of what must be and can be done in terms of transformation of policies and practices. The three points are related.

Proposals of reform of the penal system and the correctional institution abound. Dozens of reports of parliamentary committees, independent authorities, consensus conferences, criminology experts, and human rights organizations are full of useful observations and insightful recommendations. My contribution is not to add one more volume in this imposing and necessary library. What I have tried to do is to open a breach in the sum of self-evidence that has allowed the unbounded expansion of the social institution by which contemporary society responds to the most diverse perturbations of their moral or legal order, as if, for lack of imagination or courage, they were unable to conceive of others.

To punish, philosophers and jurists argue, is to correct a wrong, repair an injustice, amend a culprit, and protect society. The ultimate legitimacy of punishment is therefore the restoration of a fair social order, which had been threatened by the incriminated act. Yet if punishment is not what we say it is, if it is not justified by the reasons we invoke, if it facilitates repeat offenses instead of preventing them, if it punishes in excess of the seriousness of the act, if it sanctions according to the status of the offender rather than to the gravity of the offense, if it targets social groups defined beforehand as punishable, and if it contributes to producing and reproducing disparities, then does it not become precisely what undermines the social order? And must we not start to rethink punishment, not only in the ideal language of philosophy and law but also in the uncomfortable reality of social inequality and political violence?

Notes

1. Claude Lévi-Strauss, *Tristes tropiques* (Paris: Plon, 1955), esp. 447–49.

2. Friedrich Nietzsche, *On the Genealogy of Morals*, trans. Walter Kaufman (New York: Vintage Books, 1989; first published in German in 1887), preface, sections 2–6.

Comments

Violence, Poverty, Values, and the Will to Punish

Bruce Western

Throughout his distinguished career, Professor Didier Fassin has pioneered an anthropology that examines the institutionalization of moral projects, of which our instruments of punishment and criminal justice are preeminent examples.

"The Will to Punish" critically examines an idealized conception of punishment that is both normative and legitimizing for our criminal justice agencies. In this idealized conception, represented by H. L. A. Hart's classic definition[1], punishment is dispensed by authorities against an offender in response to wrongdoing. Punishment, in this account, may be retributive but is cool and proportionate. It may be intended to deter or incapacitate. So strong is this idea that the links between crime and punishment, victim and offender, incarceration and justice have become natural categories through which the work of police, courts, and prisons have come to be interpreted and justified. What's immediately striking to me is that punishment in this idealized conception is described without reference to social inequality. The poverty, racial inequality, and human vulnerability that define the social space in which punitive institutions function is notably absent. Against the idealized theory, Fassin develops an alternative account. Punishment is not the righteous response of authorities to crime and criminals. It is instead the infliction of pain, administered sometimes bureaucratically, sometimes to assert order through a show of force, and typically against the least powerful segments of society. Recalling his Nietzschean title, excess punishment can even take the form of a kind of state sadism in which authorities take pleasure in the infliction of suffering.[2] Much of the power of this analysis resides in its breadth of reference, denaturalizing the connection between crime and punishment as much through the anthropology of faraway cultures as through contemporary urban ethnography. This sweeping perspective reveals that both France and the United States have arrived at a mode of governance in which the coercive power of police and prison is widely used to maintain established racial and class hierarchies. From my perspective as an empirical sociologist studying incarceration in America, with one foot in a policy school that seeks to improve the world through policy reform, Fassin's analysis is revealing and at times breathtaking in its scope. I would like to probe three areas that are opened by Fassin but in my mind remain unresolved. First, I want to address the question of violence that often sets the machinery of punishment in motion. Second, I want to talk about poverty and how it becomes the ground on which the process of punishment plays out. Third, I want to discuss the normative dimension and the values that might point beyond critique to reform.

Violence

A central task of "The Will to Punish" involves challenging the natural connection between crime and punishment. We see that punishment can happen without offending when Kalief Browder is detained for years at Rikers Island or when the police abuse young African immigrants outside their group home. "Crime does not inevitably require punishment. . . . Punishment does not necessarily result from a crime," Fassin writes. "The relation between crime and punishment is more equivocal than we commonly presume."

In America the project of punishment has taken the form of mass incarceration. Criminal justice in this era has become pervasive in the daily life of America's poor. After four decades of growing prison populations that began in the early 1970s, the U.S. incarceration rate is now five times higher than its historic average and exceeds Western European rates by a factor of five to ten.[3] As Fassin observes, the rise in U.S. incarceration produced extraordinary rates of penal confinement among African American men under forty who have dropped out of high school. In work with Becky Pettit, I estimate that in recent cohorts of African American men who dropped out of high school, around 70 percent will go to prison at some point in their lives.[4] Pervasive imprisonment represents a significant expansion of state violence in very poor, largely urban communities of color.

But the scale of state violence escalated where community violence was also extreme. The emergence of mass incarceration followed not just a period of social and political unrest in the 1960s; serious crime also grew substantially. Crime rates had always been higher in urban areas than in the suburbs and rural America, but the early 1960s ushered in an increase in crime that was to last over two decades. The national homicide rate more than doubled, from 4.5 per 100,000 in the early 1960s to its peak year of 10.2 in 1980. The increase was even larger in cities, rising for example in Chicago from 10.3 in 1960 to 25.0 in 1975. The murder rate for African Americans was 6 to 10 times higher than for whites, and Gurr found the increase in violence in the 1960s and 1970s to be associated with a disproportionate rise in black murder rates.[5] Murder rates for young black men in particular reached extremely high levels—around 150 per 100,000 in 1980—making homicide the leading cause of death among blacks ages fifteen to thirty-four by the early 1990s. It is true that the scale of punishment does not track the crime rate in lockstep, but it is equally true that the distribution of violence across the population is closely correlated with the distribution of punishment.

In a recent interview study, I approached the question of the relationship between violence and punishment in another way, asking a sample of men and women released from imprisonment in Massachusetts about their involvement in violence over a lifetime.[6] The interviews revealed the lifelong salience of serious violence for men and women who were incarcerated in state prison. In childhood, formerly incarcerated people were frequently victims and witnesses to violence. Sometimes they were injured in accidents. More commonly the interviews of the reentry study revealed reports of sexual abuse, assaults, stabbings, and shootings. Fifty percent of the sample were victims of family violence. Seventy-five percent had witnessed serious injury, and 40 percent had witnessed a violent death. In adolescence, over 90 percent of the sample were regularly involved in fighting. The respondents also reported being perpetrators of violence, particularly in adulthood. As they spoke about their adult lives, the men and women of the reentry study also spoke frequently about witnessing and being victimized by violence as they had been in childhood. In adulthood, the prison itself was a site of violence, and I heard many reports of fighting in prison, mostly among people who were incarcerated but sometimes between prison staff and the incarcerated.

There is serious violence in the social space in which punishment operates. However, it looks little like the offending imagined by criminal justice ideology. There is no bright line between victims and offenders. People who commit violence often have long histories of victimization and in many cases have also been exposed to trauma in childhood as witnesses to serious violence. Violence in the lives of those who are incarcerated is of a very contextual kind, flourishing under conditions of poverty. In these conditions, home life has often been chaotic while growing up. Neighborhood environments have often been disorderly, suffering from high rates of serious crime. Understanding the relationship between violence and punishment remains a pressing task in this context.

As the Boston prisoners described their lives, it also became clear that violence often accompanied an array of other social problems, such as drug addiction, untreated mental illness, housing insecurity, and enduring unemployment. In the absence of social policy assistance—for treatment, housing, or jobs, for instance—the process of criminalization had filled the vacuum. State violence came to be the response to community violence and many of the related problems closely linked to poverty.

Critical analysis of the institutions of punishment can often miss the salience of violence in the milieux in which the police, the courts, and the prisons do their work. In the research program on mass incarceration, for example, the social problem of violence often appears to be something of a nuisance that is skirted or minimized in analysis. James Forman and Michael Fortner offer this criticism of Michelle Alexander's *The New Jim Crow*.[7]

The question of the relationship of violence to punishment is fundamental, in part because violence is a major problem in the social spaces where criminal justice authorities operate. Fassin is right that punishment is not reducible to crime, but neither is it unrelated. Violence is a variety of social action that is ripe with the possibility of criminalization. It emerges in contexts of social policy failure and contexts of poverty. (Indeed it is this contextual character of violence that I think is entirely consistent with Fassin's observation that punishment can be imposed collectively.) In addition, the violence imagined by our apparatus of punishment is largely a fiction, and the reality requires a different policy response. I may part company with Fassin in asserting a close link between violence and punishment, but I strongly share his empirical realism. Violence as it happens on the ground diverges significantly from the criminal conduct imagined by our classical conception of punishment and the policy that flows from that.

Poverty

Throughout "The Will to Punish," readers are reminded of the powerlessness and socioeconomic disadvantage of those who are punished. Fassin provides a sustained analysis of the relationship between punishment and social structures of inequality in his discussion of "who gets punished." The issue is already foreshadowed in his observation that the "punitive function of law enforcement" is applied to "the most vulnerable groups," producing "harassment, provocations, humiliations, racist insults, undue stops, unjustified searches, abusive fines, painful handcuffing, groundless arrests," and so on. In this discussion, the distribution of punishment between the poor and the rich is driven by political choice. In part this is reflected in how penal codes are designed, punishing street crime more harshly than white-collar crime, and partly this due to the street-level politics of law enforcement.

The social structure of inequality is vitally implicated in socioeconomic gradients in punishment. Fassin sees socioeconomic disadvantage as connected to punishment in two main ways. First, criminal offenses are produced in a social context. Young men in poor neighborhoods, often unemployed, come into frequent contact with police. Frustrated with police attention, these encounters often go badly. Second, the crimes of the poor are punished more harshly. Low social status diminishes the value of freedom in the eyes of the court. For the defendant who is poor and the son of immigrants, "the verdict has more to do with what he is than what he is accused of having done," writes Fassin. Criminality in this case attaches not to the conduct but to the individual. In this account, the criminogenic conditions of poverty, official processes of criminalization, and biased policing and prosecution together lead to the overrepresentation of the poor and the disadvantaged in the criminal courts and prisons.

The criminalization of poverty requires more elaboration. An older radical criminology pointed to the threat to social order posed by the unemployed, youth, and racial minorities—what Steven Spitzer has memorably called "social dynamite."[8] From this perspective, punishment helped contain a social threat that pressed not just on public safety but more broadly on norms of conformity and order. Loïc Wacquant offered a modernized version of the theory in his account of mass incarceration. For Wacquant, "the penal system in the United States has partly supplanted and partly supplemented the ghetto as a mechanism of racial control."[9] We see echoes of the social threat perspective in Fassin's ethnographic accounts of urban policing that observe the adversarial relationship between police and the citizens with whom they interact.

But social threats might be met in a variety of ways. The punitive response is grounded in a set of cultural conditions. Fassin agrees, observing the racism and xenophobia of the French police and the emotionally hot motivation that often moves punishment into action. Alternatively, as in the case of Kalief Browder, it can be tediously bureaucratic, where the courts can appear callous and disregarding of the liberty interest of criminal defendants.

I would argue that large-scale punishment projects depend significantly on the dehumanization of the poor and the powerless. Harsh punishment requires a profound suspension of human compassion. The dehumanization of people of African origin has been studied directly in psychological research on implicit bias. Psychologists find that ape-like images are associated with African American men when study subjects are given short tests in visual perception. Distorted perception has also been found for black children, who are often perceived to be much older than they really are.[10] The tough-on-crime language of *superpredators, jungles,* and *savages* are drawing from this same well of dehumanization. In a striking formulation from the heyday of the tough-on-crime era, William Bennett and his colleagues describe a new generation of criminal superpredators: "radically impulsive, brutally remorseless youngsters . . . who murder, assault, rape, rob, burglarize, deal deadly drugs, join gun-toting gangs, and create serious communal disorders. . . . To these mean-street youngsters, the words 'right' and 'wrong' have no fixed moral meaning."[11] For Bennett, the superpredators live in a world beyond the human community.

The dehumanization on which harsh punishment rests creates a research challenge in which the depiction of poverty must reassert the human reality of the poor people who come into conflict with the law. In part this involves understanding what are often the long histories of victimization and exposure to trauma, which, in contexts of severe poverty, can not only become more likely but can go untreated. Victims and offenders are not two distinct classes, but in reality are typically one and the same.

The harsh conditions of poverty in which penal severity grows often accompanies social policy failure. Mental illness, drug addiction, learning disability—all can go untreated. Human frailty—a weakness of mind and body—is a condition of poverty and is often the context in which offending and punishment arise. Two-thirds of the Boston sample, for example, reported histories of mental illness, drug addiction, or both. Chronic pain and disease were also widespread. Registering the reality of human frailty throws a spotlight on the lived conditions of poverty and erases the bright line between victim and offender.

In addition to studying the physical and mental vulnerability of those entangled in the institutions of punishment, this effort at humanization necessarily has a positive side from which springs the impulses to leniency and mercy. Here researchers can recognize and document the loving relationships, the spontaneity, and the creativity that lie at the heart of human agency.

Again the Boston interviews richly revealed the texture of social life in the shadow of penal institutions. After incarceration the men and women faced extreme poverty and acute housing insecurity. The gap in Boston was largely filled by family. Older women—mostly mothers—played a large role housing their adult sons. The loving bonds of family support seemed fundamental to being "home," even for those who had been incarcerated many times in the past. Family life often brought the stability of meal times, conversations, intimacy, and recollections of a shared history. Of course family life could sometimes be conflictual and complicated. But the key point remains that those who live in punitive social spaces are neither reducible to violence and other crime nor defined only by the suffering induced by overpolicing and incarceration.

Values

"The Will to Punish" is a critical text. Fassin dismantles several of the conceits that suffuse punitive institutions—that punishment is meted out against an offender in response to crime, coolly and deliberately. Modern criminal justice authorities tout the values of offender accountability and public safety in this effort. We can think of these as the modern remnants of the Christian ethics that value pain for its own sake yet also concede the possibility of penance and redemption.

Fassin's alternative conception of punishment also comes with a variety of normative commitments. In calling out police for their racism, it is antiracist. By identifying the injustice of punishing the poor, it is egalitarian. Behind objections to the bureaucratization of pretrial detention or the arbitrariness of prison discipline is an insistence on the protections of legal procedure. And in pointing to the perverse pleasures of punishment, there is perhaps a suggestion of abolitionism.

If the goal of critique is to bring about change, I wonder if—in the area of justice, above all—our normative commitments must be made explicit, argued for, and studied for their implications for alternative politics and policies. In the rush to punitive criminal justice policy, public safety and offender accountability were elevated beyond values to self-evident imperatives. As Fassin rightly observes, crime victims were shoehorned into a morality play that pitted good against evil, minimizing mitigation and maximizing offender culpability. These normative commitments carried extraordinary capacity to justify, seemingly, any amount of penal severity. Missing from the political debate on crime were the counterweight values that would limit the extent and severity of punishment.

What would these alternative values look like? The National Academy of Sciences report *The Growth of Incarceration in the United States* elaborated four values that should inform penal policy.[12] From the jurisprudence of sentencing, the NAS panel argued that punishment must be proportionate. The severity of punishment should be calibrated to the severity of the crime. More than this, the panel said, with the legal scholar Norval Morris,[13] that punishment be "parsimonious." By this Morris meant that punishment should always be at a minimum, imposing the least possible pain to attain its public policy purpose. Proportionality and parsimony spoke directly to sentencing policy and were well established, if not well followed, in law.

The NAS panel added two other principles that were even more limiting. The principle of citizenship was intended to assert the human dignity of those who were punished. For the NAS report, this meant that conditions of penal confinement should be humane. Those who are imprisoned do not forfeit their fundamental membership in the social compact. To this end, penal authorities should be subject to public oversight and be publicly accountable for abuse and neglect. A positive commitment to the human dignity of the incarcerated is rare in U.S. prisons, and incentives in prison administration are geared to minimizing escapes and other controversy. Embracing a principle of citizenship would fundamentally change the operation of incarceration in the United States.

Finally, the NAS report argued for the value of social justice. Social justice asserts that public institutions should function to broadly expand the rights, opportunities, and resources for all without unduly burdening any one group. The principle of social justice was intended as a counterweight to the steep race and class inequalities in incarceration, which were never weighed in the move to punitive criminal justice policy.

The four values of the NAS report aimed to elevate the document above critique, to point the way to positive reforms. In addressing mass incarceration, the committee recommended significant reductions in prison and jail populations. This could be achieved by sentencing reforms that wound back long sentences and limited mandatory-minimum sentences. This effort was to be buttressed by community-based social policy. To advance the value of citizenship, prison authorities were urged to review the conditions of confinement, perhaps particularly solitary confinement, in which prisoners can be incarcerated for months or years at a time.

The key philosophical move is the dilution of a highly individualistic ethical system. Citizenship and social justice in particular limit penal severity by emphasizing our common status as citizens with a common humanity. I wonder if mercy and leniency will ultimately spring from these values that esteem the collective as much as the individual.

Certainly the threads of human dignity and social justice run through Fassin's analysis. The ethnographic cases reveal that interactions between citizens and authorities are shot through with unaccountability, disdain, and humiliations that offend human dignity. The costs of punishment too are often social, extending beyond the individuals singled out by authorities to entire communities. In the language of the NAS panel, French policing, for example, undermines social justice because an entire social group is penalized. In my perspective, the impact of the critiques can be magnified by explicitly naming the underlying value commitments, defending them, and exploring their implications for alternatives.

Fassin has given us a wide-ranging discussion that focuses on the essential fact of punishment—the authoritative infliction of human suffering, whose operation appears deeply threatening to the aspirations of a democratic society. Yet severe social problems abound in such societies, and this is the context in which modern punishment, at least the American variety, has flourished. In asking what punishment is, analysis should probe the real conditions of violence and the human frailty that arises in contexts of poverty. In this world fraught with moral complexity and ambiguity, a new kind of normative discussion is needed. I see this as going beyond critique to reassert the bonds of social solidarity in the face of extreme injustice and inequality. And I thank Fassin for his provocation in advancing this agenda.

Notes

1. H. L. A. Hart, "The Presidential Address: Prolegomenon to the Principles of Punishment," *Proceedings of the Aristotelian Society* 60 (1959–60): 1–26.

2. "To punish is not merely to return evil for evil; it is to produce a gratuitous suffering, which adds to the sanction, for the mere satisfaction of knowing that the culprit suffers," writes Fassin.

3. Jeremy Travis, Bruce Western, and Steve Redburn, eds., *The Growth of Incarceration in the United States: Exploring Causes and Consequences* (Washington, DC: National Academy Press, 2014).

4. Bruce Western and Becky Pettit, "Incarceration and Social Inequality," *Daedalus* 139 (2010): 8–19.

5. Tedd Robert Gurr, "Historical Trends in Violent Crime: A Critical Review of the Evidence," *Crime and Justice* 3 (1981): 295–353.

6. Bruce Western, "Lifetimes of Violence in a Sample of Released Prisoners," *RSF: The Russell Sage Foundation Journal of the Social Sciences* 1 (2015): 14–30.

7. James Forman, "Racial Critiques of Mass Incarceration: Beyond the New Jim Crow," *New York University Law Review* 87 (2012): 101–46; Michael Javen Fortner, *Black Silent Majority* (Cambridge, MA: Harvard University Press, 2015); Michelle Alexander, *The New Jim Crow: Mass Incarceration in the Age of Colorblindness* (New York: New Press, 2010).

8. Steven A. Spitzer, "Toward a Marxian Theory of Deviance," *Social Problems* 22 (1975): 638–52. See also Theodore G. Chiricos and Miriam A. Delone, "Labor Surplus and Punishment: A Review and Assessment of Theory and Evidence," *Social Problems* 39 (1992): 421–46; George S. Bridges and Martha A. Myers eds., *Inequality, Crime, and Social Control* (Boulder, CO: Westview Press, 1994).

9. Loïc Wacquant, *Prisons of Poverty* (Minneapolis: University of Minnesota Press, 2009), 155.

10. Phillip Atiba Goff, Jennifer L. Eberhardt, Melissa J. Williams, and Matthew Christian Jackson, "Not Yet Human: Implicit Knowledge, Historical Dehumanization, and Contemporary Consequences," *Journal of Personality*

and Social Psychology 94 (2008): 292–306; Phillip Atiba Goff, Matthew Christian Jackson, Brooke Allison Lewis Di Leone, Carmen Marie Culotta, and Natalie Ann DiTomasso, "The Essence of Innocence: Consequences of Dehumanizing Black Children," *Journal of Personality and Social Psychology* 106 (2014): 526–45.

11. William J. Bennett, John Dilulio, and John P. Walters, *Body Count: Moral Poverty . . . And How to Win America's War against Crime and Drugs* (New York: Simon and Schuster, 1996), 27.

12. Travis et al., *The Growth of Incarceration*, chapter 12.

13. Norval Morris, *The Future of Imprisonment* (Chicago: University of Chicago Press, 1974).

Ideal Theory and Historical Complexity

Rebecca M. McLennan

Before I begin, I'd like to say a word of thanks to Chancellor Nicholas Dirks, Martin Jay, and the rest of the Tanner Lectures committee, as well as Ellen Gobler, who miraculously wrangled the four of us to be in the same place at the same time for three consecutive afternoons. I'd also like to thank Didier Fassin and my fellow panelists, David Garland and Bruce Western: it is an honor to share the podium with three such distinguished scholars; it goes without saying that I have learned a great deal from each one of you in the past several years.

It is partly because the content of the lectures is so rich and varied that I want first to offer a reading that condenses the structure of Fassin's argument and distills what I take to be his most exigent analytical and methodological insights. In the second half of my response, I will pose three of the several "big" questions that I think Fassin's lectures, taken as whole, raise. Later I will return to some of the points that I will be able only to gloss here.

This lecture takes up the questions: Why punish? and Who is punished? Here Fassin expands upon his discussion of the inadequacies of utilitarian and retributive or Kantian philosophies of punishment, which, as he said earlier, inform commonsense and legal understandings of what punishment is and should be. Fassin scrutinizes these two schools of philosophy with a social scientist's eye, arguing for their limitations, both as normative (or ideal) theories (as theories about the grounds on which "we" *should* or *ought to* punish) and as explanatory or descriptive analyses (of why "we" do *in fact* punish). The "we" in Fassin's formulation, I take it, is supposed to denote society, a rather abstract entity, or perhaps society's dominant classes; it is a little unclear, and I would suggest that being crystalline about the identity of "we" would be helpful. Among other things, it bears directly on the "distribution" question of not only who is punished but to whom and by whom the dirty work of punishment is delegated.

A. As Fassin notes, the mutual critiques of the utilitarian and Kantian philosophies of punishment, and various attempts to combine the two, are well known, at least among students of punishment. Fassin recounts the basic grounds of disagreement, but then steps out of the philosophers' forum, and with the tools and sensibility of a historically-minded social scientist, launches three potentially devastating critiques of both theories.

   1. First, he argues that despite their apparent differences, both theories commit the cardinal sin of taking for granted something they ought to explain—that is, they take for granted a determinative linkage between crime and its punishment, by which punishment, understood as the infliction of pain of some sort (whether or not paired with some rehabilitative program), is the only conceivable response to criminal wrongdoing. As we learned in the first lecture, the assumption that painful punishment follows—and *should* follow—crime was not historically, and still is not universally, the case. Fassin here marshals a dazzling array of ethnographic, etymological, and statistical evidence to establish that plenty of people are being punished for crimes that are neither endangering society's overall happiness nor morally affronting anyone's dignity; the crimes for which a majority of people are incarcerated in France (and a sizable minority in the U.S.) have no victim

at all. Conversely, there are plenty of people whose actions constitute an attack on societal happiness or on individuals' dignity and who are not charged with crime—or, if they are charged and convicted, punished so mildly as to call into question whether they have been punished at all. The sentencing of the Appalachian coal baron Donald to one year in prison for safety violations that led to the deaths of twenty-nine coal miners exemplifies the tenuous, socially contingent link between wrongdoing and punishment.

2. Fassin's second critique is that the two philosophies of punishment "fail to represent" actual punishment and the justifications that actual people offer for punishing others; both theories fail to take and represent the world as it is. Fassin's supporting examples here are drawn from the gritty, Dostoevskian world of the contemporary housing project, the traffic court, and the prison. He convincingly establishes that the people inflicting punishment—the police patrol, the lower court judge, the prison's deputy warden and guards—do not operate according to philosophers' logic: neither the goal of maximizing the happiness of society nor righting a wrong in the Kantian sense in any obvious way motivates their actions, consciously or otherwise. Instead, Fassin argues, there are other, more properly *social* "logics" or forms of reasoning at work in these settings: in the case of the police brutalization of the young hostel men, the motivation to enforce a hierarchical, racialized social order and the pedagogical imperative to teach people their inferior place; maintaining morale and thereby keeping the peace among prison guards, at the prison disciplinary hearing; and, in the case of the judge who sentences the Roma person to six months in prison for traffic offenses, following the law (however mistaken her understanding of the law).

Utilitarian and Kantian philosophies of punishment simply ignore these other motivating logics and thereby misrepresent the punished and the punishers alike. We might pause here to object that, *actually*, Kant and Bentham and most of their philosopher-heirs do not presume to "represent" real acts of punishment in their theories at all; the point of their moral philosophy is to articulate and justify an ideal toward which the unified "we"—there goes that troubling pronoun again—should strive. But even if one were to grant this, one might ask, What good is an ideal theory if it doesn't take into account human beings as they are and as they have been made and have made themselves within the larger, historically contingent force field of politics, economics, morality, life itself?

3. Fassin's third, perhaps most intriguing critique is that utilitarian and Kantian accounts fail to consider the nonlogical and arational forces that motivate and help shape the distribution and severity of real punishment in real life. Historically contingent logics (teaching people their place, etc.) combine with what Fassin, drawing on Nietzsche, calls a "repressed drive to make suffer"—a desire to punish and to punish painfully. Fassin does not fully theorize, specify, or historicize this drive to make suffer. Although he notes that the social controls to which the drive may (or may not) be subjected are historically contingent, it is unclear whether he considers the drive *itself* innate, variable, fixed, culturally produced, or something else again. What is it, and whence does it come? Whatever the case, Fassin makes the crucial observation that, in the contemporary U.S. and France, society delegates this repressed drive to make suffer to police, correctional officers, and others. This delegation, and its consequences, I think, are worthy of deeper, more systematic analysis, and I will reflect more on this and the people to whom the dirty work of making suffer is delegated presently.

Fassin closes the section of his lecture on why people do actually punish with a particularly gruesome example drawn from the United States—that of Darren Rainey, the schizophrenic drug offender who died after prison guards locked him in a boiling hot shower in a Florida prison. This event serves as a kind of synecdoche for American punishment more generally. Although much the same drive to make suffer is at work in France and other Western democracies, Fassin, I think correctly, sees the U.S. as the most extreme example of what we might call the delegated sadism that became so commonplace in the prisons, jails, and station houses of many liberal democracies after the 1970s. Here I think it would be helpful to ask not only why punishment multiplied harsh forms throughout the liberal democratic world—something that Fassin turns to in the second half of his lecture—but also why the U.S. is far and away the most extreme in this regard. Why are brutal punishments that are "hardly imaginable in Europe," today relatively routine in the U.S.? Why are American social controls over delegated sadism apparently so much weaker—the "drive to make suffer" so much less repressed—than in other *liberal* democracies, let alone the properly *social* democracies?

B. In the second half of his lecture, Fassin argues persuasively that in order to understand the punitive turn of the past forty years, it is necessary to consider "who is punished." In seeking to understand the uneven distribution of punishment, he offers an analysis of both the political economy of mass incarceration and what he calls, building on his Nietzschean insight about the repressed drive to make suffer, its moral economy. Fassin outlines the demographics of the contemporary scene, pointing to the fact that punishment is unequally distributed in both France and the U.S. The similarities of the demographics are quite striking: 75 percent of French prisoners are working class or jobless; while the state

> is barred from keeping ethnoracial records—extraordinary by American standards—Fassin estimates that 77 percent are ethnic and racial minorities. The U.S. rates are similar, though somewhat surprisingly, ethnic and racial minorities make up at most 68 percent—not 77 percent—of the state and federal prison population. Most conspicuously, low-income black men without a college education have been overwhelmingly and disproportionately caught up in the carceral machine. Although he does not provide income or employment breakdowns for the U.S., our country is possibly worse than France: the median income for imprisoned men in the year prior to incarceration was $19,185 (state prisons), well under the national median of $41,250; for incarcerated women, it was even lower, at just $13,890. An astounding 72 percent of incarcerated women earned less than $22,000 in the year prior to incarceration.

Here I would like to draw attention to two of the most exigent questions that Fassin's lectures raised for me—areas in which we might usefully push the analysis a little deeper. The first question concerns the gendered dimensions of the punitive carceral system. The statistics show that America is again the extreme outlier: 9.3 percent of prisoners are women. By contrast, women make up just 3.2 percent of the French prison population. The 200,000 incarcerated women in the U.S. account for almost one-third of incarcerated women *worldwide*. Moreover, between 1980 and 2010 women's incarceration rates actually rose *much* faster—50% faster—than men's. And although the statistics are inconsistent, reputable studies estimate that between 4 and 10 percent of imprisoned women enter prison pregnant. On at least one estimate,[1] dating from 2013, 10,000 babies are currently born in American prisons each year. The large majority are immediately taken away from their mothers (and, by default, from what most psychologists and pediatricians think of as the relationship responsible for healthy child development) and placed in foster homes or state agencies.[2] If we project this figure of 10,000 back from 2017 to the year 2000, that is 170,000 babies born in American prisons since the turn of the century. Both the explosion in female incarceration rates and the number of babies born behind bars and put in foster care are surely an important dimension of both the political and moral economies of the new regime. One in every three foster children, according to a University of Chicago study, go on to have a "high level" of involvement with the criminal justice system, and around 14% of adult inmates in California's prisons have been in foster care.[3] The growth of female incarceration, coupled with fostering practices, comprise an important, if barely visible, way in which prisons have become self-perpetuating. Judging by what Bruce Western says in his lecture about release from prisons, the positive correlation between returning to a mother's household and staying clear of prison, gender seems likely to be a much bigger and, lamentably, little understood part of the story.

The second area where I would like to push the analysis further is Fassin's treatment and conceptualization of penal history, particularly in relation to the U.S. In short, Fassin sees a kind of linearity across 250 years that I think obscures more than it illuminates for the purposes of his own project. Fassin's basic narrative is that Enlightenment thinkers, while consciously substituting moral and educational forms of punishment for bloody chastisements, also unconsciously secularized Christian ideas about the supposed redemptive value of pain and appropriated the monastic cell as a redemptive technology. Drawing on David Rothman, Fassin tells us that the first two cellular prisons proper in the U.S.—Auburn in upstate New York and Eastern State Penitentiary in Philadelphia—exemplified this new thinking, despite their organizational differences; they became, with the help of publicists such as Alexis de Tocqueville—who, incidentally, came here originally to study prisons, not democracy—the models for European penal reform.

Fassin further argues that although the experience of incarceration was admittedly different—bloodier, more punitive, scarcely rehabilitative—within the prisons themselves, the Enlightenment-inspired ideology of penal welfarism reigned through the late nineteenth century and on into the twentieth. In the 1970s the illusion that punishment and education or rehabilitation could be combined was effectively shattered: penal policy became increasingly harsh and inequitably distributed, and retributive theories of punishment enjoyed a renaissance. The prison population underwent an "unprecedented explosion" in which poor African Americans were particularly targeted by the new regime.

Two points are worth pushing here:

1. Methodologically, there is a curious paradox in Fassin's lecture: for the historical present, Fassin demonstrates the utility of breaking ideal theory's hold on what punishment is and should be, and focuses, among other things, on how punishment works in practice: de-idealizing punishment—denaturalizing the crime/punishment dyad—allows him to see the much broader logics and the political and affective economies in which punishment actually transpires. But when it comes to the historical past, at least the two centuries prior to the 1970s, his analysis reverts to the narrowly ideational dimensions of punishment; now he offers a fairly traditional intellectual history, a history of ideas and theories. He briefly acknowledges that things on the ground in places like Auburn Prison diverged from the ideology of penal welfarism, but he does not make anything of that difference.

Obviously there is a limit to how much can be covered in a single or even two lectures. But this methodological inconsistency might be fruitfully addressed in the larger project: by scrutinizing the historical past of punishment using Fassin's expansive concept of the term—actual painful punishment of actual people whether it occurs on the street or in poor and minority neighborhoods, the prison, the courthouse, or the town square—we would be in a better position to answer some of Fassin's most important questions: To what extent did the political and moral economies of punishment change over time? Who was punished back then, and what analytical relationship might they bear, if any, to those who are punished today?

Now, if one is going to transpose Fassin's method to the more distant past—that is, to track actual punishment of actual people—in the U.S. case one would need to recover the history of the infliction of pain within the single most important disciplinary institution of the eighteenth and nineteenth centuries in America: the slave plantation. Operating as a semisovereign entity, the space in which courts originally took a "hands-off" approach, much as they have tended to in relation to the prison, the plantation falls outside the private/public spatialization (which of course is a historical construct itself) that Fassin uses in the first lecture to limit the scope of his analysis to "public" punishment. We would also need to include the highways and byways on which slave patrols exercised a delegated and brutal summary justice over the bodies and souls of enslaved black people. Moving forward in time, we would need to take into account the town squares where the lynch mobs of the not so distant Jim Crow period staged elaborate festivals of blood on and around the bodies of ex-slaves and their descendants, with a punitive brutality rivaling even the storied dismemberment and execution of that failed eighteenth-century regicide, Damiens. Applying Fassin's method of "heuristic comparison" to the present and past—*that* other country—can only further illuminate the questions of who is punished today, why, and with such severity.

In such a temporally-oriented heuristic comparison, I would add to the slave plantation and its heirs the nineteenth-century American prison. These prisons did develop in certain critical respects on quite a different trajectory—both subjectively and objectively—to the French and British versions. Recall that waterboarding and other shock tactics were invented, distributed, informally standardized, and delegated in nineteenth-century American prisons. From the earliest years of the grand American experiment of cellular incarceration, excessive punishment flourished in both the nation's northern factory prisons and its southern convict lease camps; such treatment—including the whipping of prisoners, regardless of race—was even at one point legislated, not just practiced de facto, in northern, mostly white prisons. [4]

In light of this temporal comparison, we would probably have to revise our assessment of today's harsh, inequitably distributed regime as, in the words of Fassin, unprecedented. We might even have to revise the well-accepted view (to which I myself have subscribed) that the explosion in the rates of imprisonment was unprecedented—most conspicuously, far deadlier forms of carceral and noncarceral, especially of black people, exploded after the defeat of America's second revolution: Reconstruction. And it is Fassin's tremendously insightful reconceptualization and expansion of what punishment is that makes it possible to theorize the linkages between the deep and more recent past.

2. The final line of inquiry that could be fruitfully pushed further, and perhaps more broadly, is the historical and/or genealogical role of Christianity and the study of what Fassin called in his first lecture, with echoes of Carl Schmitt, penal theology. Reading Fassin's lectures, I wished for a more vigorous account of the secularization of Christian doctrine and monastic technologies of the self, and their survival and apparent dominance in today's punitive world. As a broad claim about Christianity as a crucial source of our supposedly secular system of punishment, I find it broadly persuasive. But Christian theology and practice, particularly in the early modern period and more so in recent history, were far from uniform. Particularly in the U.S. there was and is considerable variation and profound disagreement among Christian theologians, particularly on questions of crime and punishment. A couple of brief examples will suffice to demonstrate the

> possible significance of this variation for the study of penal theology. First, in the early days of the U.S. republic, many Calvinist and Congregationalist theologians and parishioners rejected the groundbreaking early penitentiary projects advocated by Benjamin Rush and others, on the grounds that to substitute the physical segregation of convicted offenders in a place designed to induce spiritual transformation (i.e., a penitentiary) was to diverge from scripture's prescriptions for punishment. Most particularly, they argued, the newfangled penitentiary transgressed Paul's admonition to rebuke sinners before the community. Worse, by undertaking to carry out a spiritual transformation of the inmate, the penitentiary was, they said, a blasphemy against God and man. Second, the Social Gospel movement of the late nineteenth and early twentieth centuries explicitly rejected pain and, interestingly, the master-servant relationship as having any place in punishment, or the classroom, the workplace, or even the family. And this particular strain of theology turned out to be tremendously influential in American penological circles during the Progressive Era.

Christian theology, in other words, was and remains neither univocal nor homogenously supportive of a harsh, retributive justice. At the same time, however, it is worth emphasizing that certain commonalities cut across otherwise heterogenous Christian value systems: we can point to many examples of the ways in which the conditions and consequences of mass incarcercation diverge from or flat-out contradict certain basic tenets of Christianity that are generally shared among otherwise disparate theologies. Take, for example, the foundational Christian (and Jewish) principle of individual moral culpability: "Fathers shall not be put to death because of their children, nor shall children be put to death because of their fathers. Each one shall be put to death for his own sin" (Deut. 24:16). This of course is the same principle that liberal law secularized, in the early modern era, as the culpable, rights-bearing subject. Then consider the awful effects of harsh punishment not only on individual prisoners but on their families, their communities, and subsequent generations. Our present system demonstrably turns this widely-subscribed—and originally religious—principle on its head. In this regard, at least, the system we *actually* have, ought to offend even the strictest retributive theorist, and certainly all the rest of us.

Notes

1. Maya Schenwar, "Female Prisoners' Babies Shouldn't Be Sentenced to Life without Breast Milk," *Guardian*, October 22, 2013.

2. Sarah Yager, "Prison Born," *The Atlantic*, July–August 2015.

3. Mark E. Courtney et al., "Midwest Evaluation of the Adult Functioning of Former Foster Youth: Outcomes at Age 19," Chapin Hall Center for Children at the University of Chicago, May 2005, cited in California Office of Senate Research, State Survey of California Prisoners: What Percentage of the State's Polled Prison Inmates Were Once Foster Care Children? December 2011, pp 1–2.

4. Rebecca McLennan, *The Crisis of Imprisonment: Protest, Politics, and the Making of the American Penal State, 1776–1941* (New York: Cambridge University Press, 2008), Chapter 3.

The Rule of Law, Representational Struggles, and the Will to Punish

David W. Garland

It is a genuine pleasure to comment on Professor Didier Fassin's Tanner Lectures, not least because he addresses questions of punishment with an intellectual and moral seriousness that is quite rare. I especially like the fact that he seeks to ground his normative analysis within an empirical understanding of penal practice—an approach that is, for me, a fundamental requirement of serious, critical work.[1] If, in what follows, I offer criticism of Fassin's claims and conclusions, these disagreements should be understood not as fundamental objections but as so many attempts to refine a contribution that I consider important and original.

I will direct my comments to the critique of punishment that Fassin has been developing over the course of his two lectures. That critical analysis is, I would say, directed less to "the will to punish" of his title than to the unlawful or illegitimate uses of violence, repression, and penal power on the part of state officials, whether police, prison staff, or judges. (Had he been undertaking his research here in the U.S., he would undoubtedly have included prosecutors, above all, federal prosecutors, in his critique, since they too wield power in an excessive and largely unrestrained manner.)

Zones of Illegality

Fassin focuses his analysis on the multiple zones of illegality where "punishments" are administered by state officials to an extent and in circumstances that exceed what the law explicitly permits. He employs ethnographic research—observing police and prison staff up close, over time, within their social worlds—as a means of bringing the margins of extrajudicial penal power back into the center of our understanding. His critical analysis is based on the claim that we ought to include these low-visibility practices in our account of the reality of punishment and on an insistence that we refer to this reality when we theorize about the nature of punishment. What ties together the series of ethnographic analyses that he presents, along with the genealogy of the concepts of punishment and pain that he develops, is the cumulative roles these play in deconstructing the conventional, legal conception of what punishment is—a conception that largely coincides with a famous definition that appears in the work of the legal scholar H. L. A. Hart.[2]

Fassin deploys this analytical strategy—restoring the margins to the center, deconstructing the lawyer's definition, showing law's repressive power is extended by unlawful but routine official practices—to develop a powerful critique: a critique of the state's use of force; a critique of signification practices that define as criminal the victims of unlawful punishment; and a critique of the immunity extended to crimes committed by criminal justice officials.

All of this is, of course, urgently topical here in the U.S., despite the fact that Fassin's field research began a decade ago and was chiefly conducted in France. Fassin's analysis goes directly to the fundamental issues raised by the police killing of suspects and civilians—Michael Brown in Ferguson, Eric Garner on Staten Island, Tamir Rice in Ohio, Walter Scott in South Carolina, among so many others. And it links directly to the efforts of groups such as Black Lives Matter that challenge the de facto immunity from prosecution that such killings have hitherto enjoyed.

Fassin's work also finds a powerful resonance at the University of California, Berkeley, with its powerful body of "law and society" scholarship. Those of us who know Malcolm Feeley's landmark work, *The Process Is the Punishment*, will recognize many of the practices that Fassin describes, most notably the use of detention awaiting trial as a mechanism for forcing guilty pleas and delivering punishment prior to any formal verdict.[3] And those of us who cherish the intellectual legacy of the great Philip Selznick will appreciate that in the background of Fassin's work stands the normative enterprise that Selznick pursued throughout his life: the project of extending legality beyond the courts in order to ensure that power, wherever it is executed, is subjected to the governance of rules.[4]

In the struggle to impose legality, a necessary first step is to render visible all those sub rosa powers that are exercised without accountability, without review, and without legal restraint—and this is an important aspect of Fassin's contribution. In pursuing his critical project, Fassin succeeds in opening up several lines of inquiry that ought to be pursued in the history and sociology of punishment. If he is correct in his claim that penal institutions routinely impose punishments that go beyond those stipulated by law, then these forms of penal excess should become part of our object of analysis. Nor is this simply the familiar realist injunction to study "law in action" and not just "law in the books";[5] it is a claim that the state's penal violence routinely exceeds that which is ostensibly permitted by law, without itself attracting legal sanction.

If we adopt Fassin's approach, we would insist, for example, that any study of the history and sociology of capital punishment in the U.S. ought to include in its observational field the history of popular lynchings that were such a feature of southern counties between 1890 and 1940. As researchers have shown, these lynchings were often death penalties, lawfully imposed, even if the law in question was local popular justice—a race law that was at odds with the laws of the state and federal government but that was nevertheless tolerated by officials.[6] Similarly Fassin's approach implies that anyone studying the meaning of imprisonment today ought to understand that the "deprivation of liberty" referenced by the law is always supplemented by pains of confinement that entail a bodily violence in excess of anything the law explicitly envisages or authorizes.[7]

Like all important work, Fassin's analyses have the potential to be generative, opening up new questions for historical and comparative research. In the wake of his research we will want to ask, for example, whether the use of police force or prison violence has varied over time. (My guess would be that, despite the current focus on the problem of police killings and police brutality, such practices are probably less extensive today than they were a generation ago, when another Berkeley sociologist—Jerome Skolnick—published his pathbreaking analysis of tolerated illegality in police practice.)[8] We will want to ask how penal violence varies from place to place; for example, are American officials more prone to penal excess than their colleagues in Canada or Europe? And how does the U.S. compare to nations such as Brazil, Argentina, or India, where extrajudicial executions and "executive killings" have sometimes been commonplace? These are important historical and comparative questions that are only now beginning to be addressed.[9]

These opening have indicated the importance of Fassin's analyses and their capacity to open up new lines of research. But having stipulated that Fassin's claims are serious and worthy of close attention, I will now proceed to develop a series of critical objections to them. And in the interests of clarity and dialectical precision, I will state these objections as sharply as possible.

Interpretive Disputes

Fassin builds his deconstructive critique of the standard jurisprudential account of punishment by citing a series of ethnographic cases and offering closely argued interpretations of them. Proceeding in this decidedly lawyerly manner, he constructs interpretative accounts of events that he and other anthropologists have observed in their ethnographic research and also of journalistic case reports that he takes from sources such as the *New Yorker* and the *Miami Herald*. But Fassin's interpretive choices are not unimpeachable, and

I will present a series of alternative readings that interpret these cases rather differently. As I will show, these alternative readings have important implications for Fassin's larger claims.

Let me begin with the best-known of the ethnographic cases, the one reported in a classic study by the Polish anthropologist Bronislaw Malinowski.[10] This is the story of the young Trobriand Islander who was conducting a sexual relationship with his cousin and who, being denounced by his cousin's former lover, killed himself in a ceremonial suicide by throwing himself from a tree. Fassin interprets the youth's incestuous affair as a crime, but he insists that it was "a crime without a punishment" because there is evidence to suppose that the youth's violation of the incest taboo was, in fact, known and tolerated prior to the outburst of the girl's discarded lover.

I would like to raise some objections to this interpretation of the facts and the legal-theoretical inferences that Fassin derives from them. Fassin says we are dealing with a crime—the breach of the incest prohibition—but this turns out to be a crime that was not punished, and he draws a number of inferences from this characterization. However, I would suggest that the norm in question can be better understood as a more subtle, situational one than Fassin suggests: a norm specifying a conditional crime that was conditionally punished.

Instead of thinking of the ban on sexual relations between cousins as an absolute prohibition, we should view it as a more conditional rule that might be fully stated as follows: "An incestuous affair may be tolerated so long as it is discreet, but must be punished if it comes to public attention." Norms of this kind are by no means exotic or unheard of. On the contrary, they are all too familiar to us, since it was this kind of rule that governed the service of gay men and lesbians in the U.S. military between 1993 and 2011: the notorious law of "Don't ask, don't tell."

I would argue that the Trobriand case does not point, as Fassin suggests, to "a crime without a punishment." It is instead a prohibition directed to public but not private conduct. The young Trobriand man was publicly shown, by his cousin's jilted lover, to be offending against the incest prohibition. The publicity "completed" the crime, with the consequence that punishment would follow. In these changed circumstances, the young man forestalled his punishment by committing suicide. There was indeed a crime, and there would indeed have been a punishment.

My second objection to Fassin is also a disagreement about the meaning of a case—this time of an American case that he interprets as an example of a "a punishment without a crime" and from which he again draws critical inferences about the inadequacy of our conventional understanding of punishment.

This is the case described in a well-known *New Yorker* article by the journalist Jennifer Gonnerman that tells the tragic story of a young man named Kalief Browder.[11] Gonnerman, and Fassin, tell us that Browder was detained in Rikers Island jail for more than a thousand days, awaiting trial for stealing a backpack—a trial that never occurred because the charges were dropped. Browder was eventually released after nearly three years, only to take his own life shortly after. Fassin calls this "a punishment without a crime and uses it, as he had done with the Malinowski vignette, to deconstruct another of the conceptual components that constitute the standard jurisprudential definition of legal punishment.

Again I would beg to differ about the meaning of the case and its implications for thinking about punishment. I certainly share Fassin's outrage that a young person should be detained in appalling conditions for an unconscionable period of time simply because (as seems to have been the case) he had a prior probation sentence and his family could not afford to post bail on his behalf. And I agree that, if the journalist's account of the facts is correct, the New York City court system, together with Browder's utterly ineffective court-appointed defense lawyer, bears a heavy moral responsibility for the young man's death. Had the Bronx courts been properly funded and functioning efficiently, no one would ever have had to wait so long to be tried. And a system of bail that is geared to socioeconomic class rather than to flight risk and public danger is a standing moral affront to any legal system. In short, I tend to share Fassin's moral response to this tragic story. But was it really "a punishment without a crime," as Fassin concludes from his analysis?

There was, we know, an alleged crime. A Mexican immigrant reported to the police that he had been assaulted and robbed of a backpack that contained seven hundred dollars, a digital camera, and credit cards. And a grand jury affirmed an indictment against Browder, charging him not with "taking a backpack," as the *New Yorker* headline puts it, but with robbery and assault. (Had no charges been brought following the Mexican man's victimization, one could imagine a different *New Yorker* story revealing that violent crimes against immigrants are being disregarded by the New York City authorities.) That these criminal charges were subsequently dropped —following the victim's return to Mexico, which made it impractical for the prosecution to have him appear as a witness—does not, except on the most formalistic, lawyerly reading of events, mean that no crime actually occurred.

And is it true that Browder—along with millions of other inmates who each year spend time in jail awaiting trial—was being "punished," as Fassin claims? Common sense says yes. The law, however, says no: he was merely being detained, and there is an important difference, though not one that Fassin appears to accept. Fassin sums up his argument here by saying that "if one takes seriously the assertion according to which a person accused of a crime is innocent until proven guilty," then everyone detained awaiting trial is being punished while innocent! But it seems to me that Fassin cannot have it both ways. If he relies on an abstruse legal formalism to claim that there was no crime and that Browder was innocent, presumably he should follow that same formalism to accept that detention on remand is not a punishment. Instead his argument combines a legal fiction—innocent until proven guilty—with a commonsense notion that detention awaiting trial is punishment.

This, it seems to me, is a questionable rhetorical conceit. Why? Because "innocent until proven guilty" is not an empirical description, sound common sense, or a statement of the facts. It is instead a legal fiction that is designed to operate as an important procedural safeguard. Speaking factually and outside of law's scheme of things, the great majority of people who are indicted for crimes are, in fact, the perpetrators of criminal acts. To imagine that our jails are full of factually innocent people is pure fantasy. It mistakes the tragic exception for the general rule. The chief problem with American criminal law is not that it indicts and detains innocent individuals, as Fassin seems to suggest. The problem is rather that it criminalizes too much and that it uses incarceration as a routine default instead of as a last resort.

This mistake is, I think, symptomatic of a recurring weakness in Fassin's argument. In these lectures everyone who is on the receiving end of unlawful state punishment, police violence, or penal excess is depicted as a harmless, innocent victim, sinned against but never sinning: the youth detained in Rikers, the driver whose license is suspended, the boys who are harassed by the French police, the blind boy seized by police in the neighborhood raid, the marijuana users and traffic law violators.

There is, it seems to me, a trace of romanticism here and, as Bruce Western suggested in his commentary, a reluctance to address the criminal violence that is so often intertwined with—and used to justify—penal violence. It is an easy matter to criticize and condemn the state's punishment of innocent individuals. But in the U.S. today, the more important task is to criticize the overpunishment of the guilty—including the majority of inmates in state prisons who are serving lengthy prison terms following convictions for violent offenses.

One of the distinctive background features of American society—a feature that helps explain public tolerance of police misconduct and penal excess—is the very high rates of homicide, armed robbery, and violent crime.[12] These levels of violence sharply distinguish this society from other developed nations, where homicide levels are markedly lower. And of course the chief victims of all this violence are poor black men, living in poor, minority neighborhoods.[13] Even now, after twenty years of continual declines in violent crime rates, homicide remains the leading cause of death among black males ages fifteen to thirty-four. If, as seems likely, this background fact helps shape interactions between the police and criminal suspects and between the public and penal policymakers, it should surely be accorded a place in our interpretation of the outcomes of these processes.

Representational Struggles

At various points in his lectures, Fassin alludes to the "representational struggles" that are involved in labeling an act either a punishment or alternatively an unlawful act of state violence. These struggles are of considerable importance. They shape how specific acts of violence will be perceived and defined, and they thereby affect the likelihood that such acts will be tolerated or not.

I take it that Fassin's project involves an attempt to uncover covert acts of state violence and expose them to criticism and control. (This is what I was referring to earlier when I talked of his Selznickian aim of subjecting arbitrary power to the governance of rules.) But if that is the case, then it seems to me that Fassin's analytical approach obstructs rather than furthers that critical project. It seems to me that his strategy of deconstructing the legal definition of punishment and thereby putting the very nature of state punishment into question actually diminishes our capacity to engage in the relevant representational struggles. More especially it makes it more difficult to define specific acts of state officials as being unlawful abuses of power.

The distinction that I invoke here—between lawful punishment and lawless state violence—is, I would argue, crucial to the project of extending legality and taming arbitrary state power. And it is precisely this distinction that Hart's definition of legal punishment is intended to render crisp and clear. But Fassin deploys a series of supposed instances of extralegal punishment to bring this legal definition into question—to show that the punishments meted out in the social worlds he studies do not conform to the dictates of law. Indeed his whole methodology in these lectures is to use observed instances of penal excess—of unwarranted official violence unfolding in criminal justice settings—as a means to deconstruct the legal definition of punishment. This, it seems to me, would be an effective methodology if his aim was to develop the sort of genealogical critique that is suggested by his Nietzschean title, "The Will to Punish," and by the etymological analyses he offers in his second lecture. But it seems to me that his *normative* project—which is not at all the same as a Nietzschean genealogy—should prompt him to proceed in exactly the reverse direction. If he aims to bring the state's lawless conduct into question, then he ought to demonstrate that it departs from legal punishment properly defined. Instead he cites the existence of these illegalities as a reason to blow up the legal definition, an approach that I regard as altogether counterproductive.

The existence of state practices that ignore law's restraints and impose unlawful punishments is not a reason to doubt or deconstruct the conventional definition of legal punishment. It is a reason to apply it vigorously and insist on upholding it in the representational and political struggles that, today more than ever, swirl around issues of policing and punishment.

Let me support this critical objection by pointing to the evidence that Fassin uses to rethink the concept of punishment in a way that embraces the illegal conduct of state officials.

When he describes unlawful uses of state violence as instances of authorized punishment, Fassin relies on two forms of evidence to support his account. The first is what he calls "local justifications." Examples of these are the subjective meanings of the officials who are directly involved: the police officers who retaliate against a hostile population of "offenders and accomplices"; the prison officers who sentence inmates to solitary confinement on the basis of trumped up charges that no one believes; and so on. The second evidence he points to is what he terms "broader explanations." Here he refers to the culture of the police precinct or the prison institution where such acts are routinely tolerated, justified, and excused.

Against this I would insist that there is also a *third* source of meaning, a third force in the representational struggles that address these acts and contest their meanings. This third signifying force is *the law* and the sections of the state apparatus and the political classes that insist on applying the law according to the rules of legality and according to strict definitions of legal punishment. The effect of the deconstructive critique that Fassin presents is to undercut this vital, critical force, to dilute punishment's legal definition and widen the category of punishment to include pretty much whatever state officials choose to add. My preferred approach would be to uphold the standard legal definition in its most rigorously demanding form and use it to criticize any official conduct that deviates from its norms.

Let me illustrate my point by recalling the history of popular lynching in the southern states of the U.S. in the years between 1890 and 1940.[14] For generations, local mobs would seize hold of individuals—mostly though not exclusively poor, black men—who had allegedly committed some crime or outrage and proceed to put them to death in an act of "popular justice." These mob killings were murderous acts that bore little resemblance to Hart's account of what is required for an act of punishment to be deemed lawful. And yet the mobs' leaders believed that they were imposing a deserved punishment and that they were in fact authorized to do so—a set of beliefs that was ratified by the conduct of southern sheriffs, prosecutors, coroners, and juries who refused to prosecute or convict the lynchers. What we see in these instances is the effect of "subjective meanings" and "local justifications" in defining the mob's actions as authorized punishment. And precisely because state governments and the federal authorities did nothing, and because their refusal to act was not effectively challenged by antilynching forces, it was the subjective meanings and local justifications of the lynchers that prevailed.

But over time these forms of punishment—the penal excess of the lynch mob—were increasingly subjected to external criticism and forceful challenge. A "representational struggle" ensued, and with the support of the NAACP, the American Communist Party, and eventually the federal government, these southern punishments were redefined as crimes, lynch mobs were redefined as murderers, and the perpetrators were threatened with criminal prosecution and criminal punishment. The long struggle to impose the restraints of legality on the power of local mobs—and to measure their behavior against the conventional definition of legal punishment—eventually succeeded.[15]

On June 7, 1998, in the town of Garland, Texas, James Byrd Jr., a forty-nine-year-old African American, was seized by three white men. Two of the men were white supremacists; one sported on his arm a tattoo of a black man hanging from a tree. The men tied Byrd to their pickup truck and dragged him for three miles, until his bones were broken and his head detached from his body. The white supremacists, it seems, had attempted to stage a lynching. But all three men were arrested by the local police, prosecuted by the local district attorney, and sentenced by a local jury to the penalty of death for first-degree murder. Their case can stand for the proposition that, in southern communities of the U.S., what was once a popular punishment has been redefined as a heinous crime.

Lynchings, police killings, unlawful confinements—these become de facto legal punishments when law officers and state authorities collude with their perpetrators and refrain from contesting their questionable legality. They become crimes—de facto and de jure crimes—when such collusion ends and the law is rigorously enforced. The struggle to move from the unlawful use of force to legally regulated punishments depends, in no small part, on maintaining a sharp distinction between them. For these reasons, and despite the forceful arguments of Fassin, I would suggest that critics of official misconduct would be well advised not to deconstruct Hart's definition of punishment as if it were a complacent, badly informed description; they should instead put it to the critical use for which it was always intended.

Notes

1. On the relationship between the philosophy of punishment and empirical studies of penal practice, see Antony Duff and David Garland, eds., *A Reader on Punishment* (Oxford: Oxford University Press, 1994).

2. H. L. A. Hart, "Prolegomenon to the Principles of Punishment," in *Punishment and Responsibility: Essays in the Philosophy of Law* (Oxford: Oxford University Press, 1968).

3. Malcolm M. Feeley, *The Process Is the Punishment: Handling Cases in a Lower Criminal Court* (New York: Russell Sage Foundation, 1979).

4. Philip Selznick, *Law, Society and Industrial Justice* (New Haven, CT: Yale University Press, 1964) and *The Moral Commonwealth* (Berkeley: University of California Press, 1992). And of course behind Selznick's work stands Lon L. Fuller, *The Morality of Law* (New Haven, CT: Yale University Press, 1964).

5. Roscoe Pound, "Law in Books and Law in Action," *American Law Review* 44 (1910): 12–36.

6. See David Garland, "Penal Excess and Surplus Meaning: Public Torture Lynchings in Twentieth-Century America," *Law & Society Review* 39.4 (2005): 793–833.

7. David Garland, "The Problem of the Body in Modern State Punishment," *Social Research* 78.3 (2011): 767–98.

8. Jerome H. Skolnick, *Justice without Trial* (New York: John Wiley & Sons, 1966).

9. Jerome Karabel, "Police Killings in Comparative Perspective," paper delivered at the NYU Workshop on American Punishment, October 2016.

10. Bronislaw Malinowski, *Crime and Custom in Savage Society* (London: Rowman and Littlefield, 1926).

11. Jennifer Gonnerman, "Before the Law," *New Yorker*, October 6, 2014.

12. See Lisa L. Miller, "What's Violence Got to Do with It? Inequality, Punishment and State Failure in US Politics," *Punishment & Society* 17.2 (2015): 184–210.

13. See David Garland, "American Penal Power: Its Forms, Functions and Foundations," *Journal of the British Academy* (2017) Volume 5: 1–35.

14. See generally, W. Fitzhugh Brundage, *Under Sentence of Death: Lynching in the South* (Chapel Hill: University of North Carolina Press, 1997); Stewart E. Tolnay and E. M. Beck, *A Festival of Violence: An Analysis of Southern Lynchings, 1882–1930* (Urbana: University of Illinois Press, 1995).

15. For a general discussion of the social, economic, and political circumstances that empowered this legal critique and contributed to the abolition of lynchings, see Philip Dray, *At the Hands of Persons Unknown* (New York: Random House, 2002).

Reply

What Is a Critique of Punishment?

Didier Fassin

Having my work discussed by three distinguished scholars whose writings have nourished my reflection as I was preparing these Tanner Lectures is a privilege and an honor. The three disciplines of the social sciences that they represent— sociology, history, and law—bring complementary perspectives, which productively converse with my ethnographical, genealogical, and philosophical approach. I am therefore grateful for their careful reading and penetrating comments. Their observations, suggestions, and criticisms will allow me to clarify, specify, and deepen my arguments. In response to their remarks, I want to address more broadly the question: What is a critique of punishment?

Let me start by restating my project. Most of the abundant literature on punishment quite expectedly stems from legal theory and moral philosophy and shares a common feature: a normative stance. It expounds what punishment should be, how it should be justified, and how it should be distributed. I do acknowledge the relevance and significance of this literature, of the academic debates it generates around important issues, and of the posture it adopts regarding how the penal world ought to be. This is what I have tried to convey in my punctilious exposition of the theses developed by jurists and philosophers in the past three centuries. But mine is a distinct set of interrogations. What I want to account for is what punishment actually is and what its actual justifications and distribution are. To do so, I mobilize, on the one hand, decade-long empirical research that I have conducted on three institutions directly involved in the act of punishing, namely the police, the courts, and the prison, and on the other hand, an ad hoc genealogical analysis that borrows from various philological, historical, and anthropological sources. Perhaps not surprisingly, the result of this inquiry is that punishment is not what it is supposed to be, that the logics from which it proceeds considerably exceed its alleged justifications, and that the inequality that underlies it profoundly contradicts its ideal distribution.

My critical approach to punishment is therefore fundamentally grounded in the classical confrontation between "ought" and "is," but instead of contesting, as Hume does, that an "ought" could be derived from an "is," I somewhat symmetrically question the fact that an "ought" could be taken for granted as an "is." Too often politicians, judges, journalists, and more broadly the public insensibly shift from the prescriptive to the putatively descriptive and, for instance, tend to believe that a punishment is simply what it ought to be, namely the infliction of pain, within a legal framework, on an offender for the offense he has presumably committed. Conversely, I provide multiple examples in which at least one of these criteria is absent—because there is no offense, because there is no evidence about the offender, or because there is no legal framework—pointing out that the only constant is the imposition of some form of suffering. But I want to avoid misunderstandings. I am not asserting that actual punishment never corresponds to its normative definition; it often does, and I repeat this point on several occasions. Rather I am affirming that not infrequently it does not match the definition and that in such cases it is crucial to still view it as punishment. But this assertion is far from new, and I must acknowledge the precedents of Malcolm Feeley and Philip Selznick, whose important writings on the functioning of the justice system in the United States I discovered only after having already delivered these lectures.

The same reasoning on "ought" and "is" holds for justification and distribution. Indeed neither utilitarianism nor retributivism, which are the two common theories used to justify punishment, suffice to account for the multiple reasons one punishes in the street, in court, or in jail. Similarly the assumption that the distribution of punishment should be just and fair is definitely contradicted by empirical evidence, which shows that sentences are neither proportionate to the seriousness of the crime nor equitably allocated across society. It is therefore essential to acknowledge this substantive difference between "ought" and "is." However, critique must not stop here. It must offer an interpretation of this difference. What does it tell us about the contemporary world? This is what I try to do by showing, first, that the equivalence established between punishment and infliction of pain is the historical outcome of the shift from reparation to suffering; second, that beyond the rational arguments provided to justify the imposition of punishment there remains an obscured dimension of pleasure; and third, that socioracial disparities in the distribution of punishment consolidate and legitimize inequality within society.

To this critical approach to punishment my discussants make two important objections: one is general and concerns the normative assumptions it involves; the other is more specific and pertains to a vindication of the normative definition.

According to Bruce Western, my critique is not exempt from commitments to certain values. I cannot but agree with this statement, which is to some degree largely true for any sort of critique, especially when it addresses moral issues. Even if I attempt to be strictly descriptive in the ethnographical account and analytical in the genealogical exploration, both endeavors are underlain by implicitly normative assumptions regarding inequality, discrimination, and cruelty. The very choice of these terms implies a disapproval of the social facts that they designate, little sympathy for those who contribute to their production, and adherence to values of social justice, dignity, and humaneness. But even if neither of the two approaches is value-free, there is an essential difference between saying that punishment should be just and fair (what jurists and philosophers do) and establishing the existence of disparities in the allocation of punishment and examining the mechanisms that explain them (what social scientists do). The former position is prescriptive; the latter is descriptive. Thus I avoid proposing policies and programs, abolitionist or other, contrary to what Western suggests, considering that my role is instead to provide the most accurate and relevant critical analysis possible for a public discussion on what must be changed in the way we punish. Such transformation cannot be the sole prerogative of social scientists. Deciding what should be is incumbent upon citizens—and among them, social scientists. It is not unreasonable to think that the critique of prison as an institution currently undermined by its inefficacy and unfairness can contribute to some conversion of "is" into "ought" in the public: to wit, a political questioning of carceral inflation.

For David Garland, my critique of punishment is misplaced because I should accept the legal definition, and when facts do not correspond to it, simply dismiss them as irrelevant. For instance, when the police brutally arrest working-class youth belonging to racial minorities, when the judge remands in custody an impecunious defendant to force his admission of a putative offense, or when the prison disciplinary board sentences an inmate without being convinced of his culpability, I should not view their actions as punishment since they do not fit the legal definition, even if the agents inflicting the ordeal, those subjected to it, and a good part of the public more or less explicitly see these actions as forms of punishment. In Garland's view, the first case should be regarded as unlawful state violence, the second one as well-founded detention, and the third one as abuse of power. This is a classical Durkheimian position: the sociologist defines his object a priori and rejects facts that do not meet his definition. It is also a legalistic stance: the lawyer has the law for absolute reference. By contrast, I have a Weberian inclination, giving importance to the way people give sense to their action, and an anthropological posture, which pays attention to the natives' point of view, be they police officers, judges, guards, youths, or the public. But being a Durkheimian sociologist and a lawyer—both qualities that are highly respectable—Garland logically sticks to H. L. A. Hart's definition. Or rather he retains only what the British philosopher calls "the standard case," which corresponds to the official delineation of punishment, while ignoring Hart's crucial warning about the danger of using it as a "definitional stop," that is, as a way of excluding what does not conform with the standard case. Why is such restrictive reading dangerous? Precisely because it "would prevent us from investigating the very thing which modern skepticism must call into question": the way punishment has been normalized. In other words, for Hart, dismissing what does not fit the ideal definition would preclude any foundational critique of punishment. Indeed police violence would appear to be a mere deviance instead of being a common way of dispensing justice in the street in compensation for the judges' supposed leniency and with the blessing of the authorities and the public; detention awaiting trial would be regarded as a simple application of the law even if the painful and often cruel consequences of such a decision are used by the judge as a means to pressure the defendant, and imposed only on the poor unable to pay the bail; and sentencing to solitary confinement without evidence of any violation of the rules would become a dysfunction of the correctional system rather than a method of maintaining order via discretionary retribution. The decision to adopt a strict definition or, conversely, to put the definition to the test of actual situations undeniably pertains to a "representational struggle," as Garland correctly argues, and it has considerable implications for what the critic sees and what critique means, but also for what can be done to improve the penal system and correct its most problematic flaws. I would certainly not dispute his point that law has the power to define what is lawful punishment and what is unlawful violence, as in the case of lynching, which he brings as his final example, and both legislators and courts do have a role to play in establishing and implementing this distinction. But in a time when the power of law often serves to protect the powerful and when its enforcement frequently means the enforcement of a social order by disciplining the dominated segments of society, I would also call for a necessary critique of the law, in particular for its biased, reductive, and predetermined definition of punishment.

Interestingly the position adopted by Rebecca McLennan is almost symmetrical to Garland's standpoint. Instead of contesting the reopening of the definition of punishment, she invites me to pursue my critical approach even further, by extending it more broadly to the modern period. In the case of eighteenth- and nineteenth-century United States in particular, what would a political economy of punishment look like, she asks, if, instead of limiting penal history to the history of the prison system, I included the institution that has served not only as a means to produce riches but also as an instrument to discipline part of the population, namely the slave plantation, as well as the extrajudicial punitive practices of the slave patrols and later lynch mobs? The question is definitely pertinent, and Loïc Wacquant has theorized the historical sequence of chattel slavery in times past, Jim Crow laws not so long ago, and mass incarceration today. Furthermore McLennan's insistence on the need to treat history both in a nonlinear way, so as to reveal the ruptures as much as the continuities, and within specific national contexts, so as to identify differences as well as similarities, is germane to my project, although I must admit that my interpretation is more genealogical than historical, mostly aiming at identifying major transformations in the moral economy of punishment.

Because these lectures deal with punishment, my analytical focus has been on the penal chain. This expression refers to the complex network of actors and actions that are involved in the punishment of certain categories of individuals for certain categories of acts that they have committed. The penal chain includes the prison system, the justice apparatus, the police forces, the legislature, the executive, political parties, and even the media and the public inasmuch as they are supposed to influence—but more often than not are influenced by—the authorities in their repressive drive; this is how "public opinion" is instrumentalized. Who is punished for what, how, and why—and who is not? This question is central to my inquiry.

But what about the actual reasons certain individuals are punished? In other words, what about crime? "There is serious violence in the social space in which punishment operates," Western rightly observes. His interviews with former prisoners attest to this violence, which they have experienced since their childhood both as victims and as perpetrators. While I have tried to show that the connection between crime and punishment, albeit generally taken for granted, was not necessary, he adds that they nevertheless often go together. I would certainly not contradict him on this point, and in my book dedicated to the ethnography of a short-stay prison I do insist on the importance of combining the analysis of the penal chain and the study of the social structure to understand what leads to the unequal distribution of crime and punishment. More specifically, in the lectures, when discussing the case of the young man of Senegalese origin accused of insulting the police and resisting arrest, I speak of the social conditions of possibility of his criminal record, referring to his dropping out of school, the economic precarity of his family, the racial discrimination he faces in the job market, and the multiple opportunities for illegal activities he encounters in his neighborhood. However, when comparing my ethnography with Western's research, I cannot emphasize too much how important it is to take into account the disparity in the levels of violence and crime between the United States and Europe. In the former, at the peak of the homicide epidemic in the 1980s, the rate was ten times higher than in most countries of the latter, and this ratio even reached one hundred times for African Americans residing in cities like Chicago. Such quantitative differences translate into qualitative discrepancies. In France, for instance, prison demographics have steadily increased since the 1980s despite a regular decrease in homicides, suggesting a clear disconnection between crime and punishment, contrary to what occurred in the United

States in the 1970s, when mass incarceration began in a context of a dramatic rise in urban violence. It is therefore crucial, when addressing these issues, to avoid the common error of generalizing on the basis of what is seen in the United States, since the situation of this country is not just the exaggeration of a punitive trend noted elsewhere; it presents specific extreme features related to its racial and violent history and sociology, which make it an outlier in the concert of nations. If parallels are to be drawn in terms of crime and punishment, Brazil, South Africa, and the Philippines may be more relevant analogies than France, Germany, or Sweden.

The analytical shift from punishment to crime is extended even further by Garland, who writes that, in my case studies, "everyone who is on the receiving end of unlawful state punishment, police violence, or penal excess is depicted as a harmless, innocent victim, sinned against but never sinning," a bias he attributes to "a trace of romanticism." However, I do not believe that the subjects I evoke in the scenes I relate are presented as harmless and innocent. The Roma man who was driving without a license had nineteen previous citations and is later reincarcerated for domestic violence; the youth of Senegalese descent who is accused of insulting the police and resisting arrest had five summonses by the age of nineteen. In the case of the blind man, he is known as a local drug dealer, but the conspicuous element is that the police who have raided his neighborhood end up realizing that he could not have been involved in the initial intervention. As for the inmate, more than thirty incidents have been reported since his imprisonment, but again the significant point is that he is sentenced to solitary confinement because of his past rather than on the basis of any evidence or even investigation regarding the present accusation. These men all have criminal records, and I am not romanticizing their fate. But my concern is not so much about their crime, which I cannot ignore of course; it is rather about their punishment. When law enforcement units rush into a housing project in search of a culprit, indiscriminately maltreat the inhabitants, and randomly arrest individuals, what interests me is that an event is occurring that is regarded by most protagonists as a punishment, although the distinction with revenge is not always clear, and that this punishment associates two typical characteristics, being collective and random, with the implication of a very high probability of innocent people receiving retribution. When children are harassed by the police in the street, when a man is incarcerated for driving without a license, and when a prisoner is kept in administrative segregation without proof of his misdeed, what interests me is that the logics behind these punishments do not match the habitual justifications for punishing. Finally, when a man is jailed on remand for a verbal altercation with police officers and another one goes home after having been convicted of sexual assault on his partner, what interests me is to understand how the social and racial elements interfere in the judge's decision to account for the discrepancy in severity. The first case questions our comprehension of what is punishment, the second of why we punish, and the third of who gets punished. I do not argue that these cases exhaust the innumerable forms of punishment, but they falsify, to use Popperian language, the normative claims of legal theory and moral philosophy. They help us rethink what we assume we know about punishment. Besides, for the social scientist as well as for the citizen, the fact that the police would harass, humiliate, and brutalize individuals with impunity, that the justice system would show more harshness toward the marijuana user than the corrupt politician, and that the correctional institution would commonly debase, abuse, and strip inmates of their rights, may be a concern worth considering—even if those who are affected by these various mistreatments are neither "harmless" nor "innocent" victims. I believe this is also what Garland means when he appropriately writes that "the more important task is to criticize the overpunishment of the guilty." I would simply add that this criticism should not be limited to their "serving lengthy prison terms" but should also include a more qualitative dimension: that of the violence inflicted by the multiple public institutions that have dealings with them.

If people are treated in this way, it is because of their social condition and what it seems to authorize, argues Western: "large-scale punishment projects depend significantly on the dehumanization of the poor and the powerless." Once dehumanized, or at least demeaned, it becomes much easier to bully, torment, and crush them. He evokes in particular the "tough-on-crime language of *superpredators, jungles,* and *savages.*" These are the exact same words that were often employed by my interlocutors during my fieldwork with police units. But conspicuously I never heard any such designation during the four years of my research in prison, a difference that I have interpreted as being due to the guards' closer relationship with and better knowledge of their public, despite the fact that the latter is similar to that of law enforcement officers. Again this finding seems to depart from what is reported about prison life in the United States. An essential implication of Western's analysis is that social scientists have a responsibility in transforming the image of the poor and the powerless, who often belong to ethnoracial minorities, in order to rehumanize them, so to speak. This is what ethnography can do, not as part of a moral mission to make people look better but simply as a consequence of a methodological project seeking to account for their social life as human beings.

One crucial aspect of this social life is what McLennan calls "the gendered dimensions of the punitive carceral system," and she insists on the formidable increase in female carceral demographics: "almost one-third of incarcerated women *worldwide*" are held in the United States, two-thirds of them being mothers of a minor child, and ten thousand of them giving birth every year in correctional facilities. These striking figures, which once more affect the most disadvantaged parts of the population—black and Hispanic women representing almost half of those incarcerated, a proportion two times greater than in the general population—highlight the impact of today's repressive trend on the next generation and, to a large extent, announce the social reproduction of crime and punishment, as more than eight million children have at least one parent in prison or under correctional supervision in the United States. The deleterious long-term effects of the punitive moment on a society cannot be better expressed.

Having spent ten years studying the police, justice, and prison systems through ethnographic lenses that have given me important empirical as well as theoretical insights on the repressive system in France and beyond, I have felt the need to continue my reflection on the broader issue of punishment. To do so I have attempted a dual shift—temporal and spatial. Most of the research produced on this topic focuses on a relatively limited period, between a few decades and the past three centuries, and on one country, the United States; it is indeed the case for my interlocutors, although they all come, just like me, from other parts of the world, namely New Zealand, Australia, and Britain. The genealogical inquiry has allowed me to explore other regions of time and space. In parallel I have tried to put to the test normative theories, legal and philosophical. Not that I would question their validity, but I felt that they restrained our comprehension of actual phenomena by foreclosing certain interrogations and forbidding certain investigations—as my discussants acknowledged, even when they disagreed with my tentative proposals. The ethnographic approach has allowed me to reopen the field of possibilities.

The heterodox method that I have used has for its main raison d'être unsettling self-evidence and initiating a debate. From this perspective, the exchanges I have had with my three colleagues have definitely been enthralling and rewarding. But my intention in delivering these lectures and translating them into a book was to go beyond academic circles. It was to engage in a public discussion about the punitive moment and the danger it presents for contemporary societies. The publication of the French version, *Punir: Une passion contemporaine*, at the beginning of 2017 has been an opportunity to have some of the issues raised in my work debated in numerous fora, from newspapers to radio and television broadcasts, from human rights organizations' meetings to political parties' programs, from workshops with judges to conferences with correctional administrators, from encounters with inmates and guards in prison to public talks at cultural events. Considering the quasi-absence of the topic during the recent French presidential campaign, the outcome has certainly been modest. But it is my belief that these questions engage our present and future, and as such need to be discussed as widely as possible. To paraphrase Georges Clémenceau's famous remark about war and the military at the end of the nineteenth century, punishment is too important to be left to the lawyers and criminologists.

Index

The manufacturer's authorised representative in the EU for product safety is Oxford University Press España S.A. of El Parque Empresarial San Fernando de Henares, Avenida de Castilla, 2 - 28830 Madrid (www.oup.es/en or product.safety@oup.com). OUP España S.A. also acts as importer into Spain of products made by the manufacturer.
Printed and bound by CPI Group (UK) Ltd, Croydon, CR0 4YY
14/09/2026
02216290-0001